GRADE 2

100 Math Practice Pages

New York • Toronto • London • Auckland • Sydney
Mexico City • New Delhi • Hong Kong • Buenos Aires

Teaching Resources

Text Credits: Practice Pages 3–5, 7, 14, and 45 taken and/or adapted from *Solve-the-Riddle Math Practice* by Liane B. Onish © 2009 by Liane B. Onish; Practice Pages 17, 20, 22, 25, 34, 37, 42, 50, 52, and 54 taken and/or adapted from *Solve-the-Riddle Math Practice: Addition & Subtraction* by Liane B. Onish © 2010 by Liane B. Onish; Practice Pages 66, 69, 74, 77, and 83 taken and/or adapted from *Solve-the-Riddle Math Practice: Time & Money* by Liane B. Onish © 2010 by Liane B. Onish; Practice Pages 19, 27, 43, 47, and 57 taken from *50 Fill-In Math Word Problems: Addition & Subtraction* by Bob Krech and Joan Novelli © 2009 by Bob Krech and Joan Novelli; Practice Pages 6, 29, 31, 56, 62, 80, and 88 taken from *Activities for Fast Finishers: Math* by Jan Meyer © 2010 by Jan Meyer; Practice Pages 18, 33, 40, 46, 49, 60, and 85 taken and/or adapted from *Practice, Practice, Practice! Addition & Subtraction* by Betsy Franco © 2005 by Betsy Franco; Practice Pages 58, 61, 63, 65, 68, 71, 75, and 78 taken and/or adapted from *Practice, Practice, Practice! Time, Money & Measurement* by Christine Hood © 2015 by Christine Hood; Practice Pages 10, 39, 84, 89, and 100 taken and/or adapted from *Tic-Tac-Math: Grades K–2* by Sue Hansen © 2005 by Sue Hansen; Practice Page 55 adapted from *Tic-Tac-Math: Grades 3–4* by Matthew Friedman © 2005 by Matthew Friedman. Other Practice Pages from this workbook were previously published in: *Math Picture Puzzles for Little Learners*; *Math Problem of the Day Practice Mats*; and *Morning Jumpstarts: Math, Grade 2*.

Edited by Mela Ottaiano
Cover design by Lindsey Dekker
Interior design by Melinda Belter

ISBN: 978-0-545-79938-6
Compilation copyright © 2015 by Scholastic Inc.
Illustrations copyright © by Scholastic Inc.
All rights reserved.
Published by Scholastic Inc.

4 5 6 7 8 9 10   40   22 21 20 19 18

Contents

Introduction

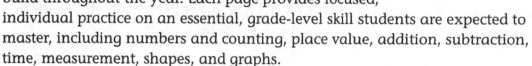

In today's busy classrooms, it is vital to maximize learning time. That's where *100 Math Practice Pages, Grade 2* comes in. The activities in this book are designed to review and reinforce a range of math skills and concepts students will build throughout the year. Each page provides focused, individual practice on an essential, grade-level skill students are expected to master, including numbers and counting, place value, addition, subtraction, time, measurement, shapes, and graphs.

Reviewing concepts students have already learned is a good way to keep their math skills sharp and to discover where revisiting a skill may be beneficial. You know your students best, so feel free to pick and choose among the activities and incorporate them as you see fit. The goal is to build automaticity, fluency, and accuracy so students succeed in school.

How to Use This Book

Preview each activity page to ensure that students have the skills needed to complete it. If necessary, walk through its features with your class to provide an overview before you assign it and to make sure students understand the directions. Work out a model problem or two as a class.

The 100 practice pages can be used to enhance the curriculum during math time, to keep fast finishers on task anytime, or as homework.

You'll find an answer key beginning on page 107. If time allows, you might want to review answers with the whole class. This approach provides opportunities for discussion, comparison, extension, reinforcement, and correlation to other skills and lessons. Your observations can direct the kinds of review or reinforcement you may want to add to your lessons. Alternatively, you may find that having students discuss activity solutions and strategies in small groups is another effective way to deepen understanding.

The engaging activity pages are a great way to help students:

✓ reinforce key academic skills and concepts

✓ meet curriculum standards

✓ prepare for standardized tests

✓ succeed in school

✓ become lifelong learners

Meeting the Standards

Completing the exercises will help students meet the College and Career Readiness Standards for Mathematics, which serve as the backbone for the practice pages in this book. These broad standards were developed to establish a framework of clear educational expectations meant to provide students nationwide with a quality education that prepares them for college and careers. The following list details how the activities in this book align with the standards in the key areas of focus for students in grade 2.

Standards for Mathematics

MATHEMATICAL PRACTICE

1. Make sense of problems and persevere in solving them.

2. Reason abstractly and quantitatively.

3. Construct viable arguments and critique the reasoning of others.

4. Model with mathematics.

5. Use appropriate tools strategically.

6. Attend to precision.

7. Look for and make use of structure.

8. Look for and express regularity in repeating reasoning.

MATHEMATICAL CONTENT

✓ Operations and Algebraic Thinking

✓ Number and Operations in Base Ten

✓ Measurement and Data

✓ Geometry

Name _____   Date _____

Beautiful Butterfly

If the number matches	Color the space
Twenty	Yellow
Forty	Green
Sixty	Blue
Eighty	Orange
One hundred	Purple

Color Key

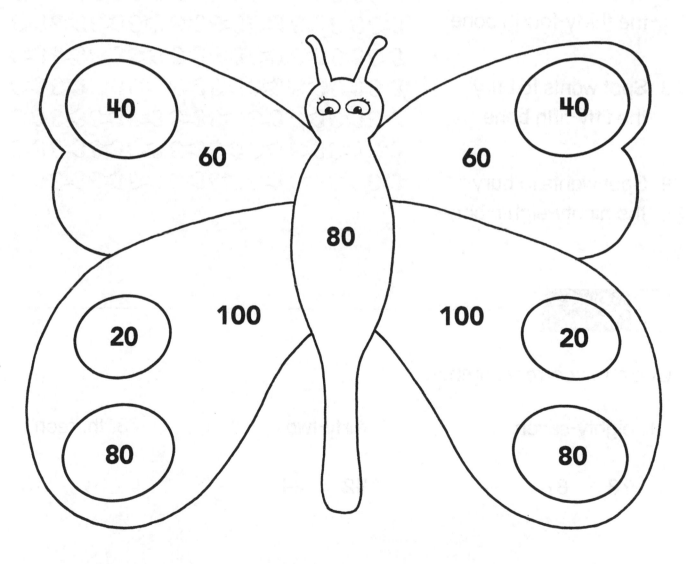

100 Math Practice Pages, Grade 2 © 2015 • Scholastic Teaching Resources

Spot the Bone

Help Spot the Dog spot his favorite bones.
Read the sentences below.
Circle the bones Spot wants to bury.

1. Spot wants to bury
   the twelfth bone.

2. Spot wants to bury
   the thirty-fourth bone.

3. Spot wants to bury
   the fifty-fifth bone.

4. Spot wants to bury
   the ninety-eighth bone.

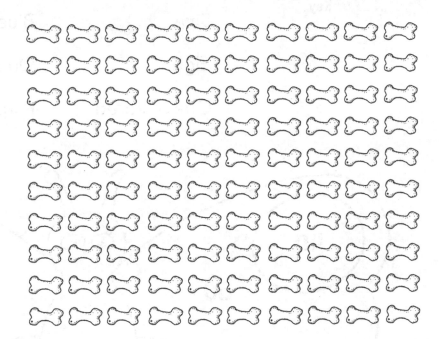

 **Quick Review**

Circle the correct number.

1. eighty-seven

    78   87

2. forty-two

    42   24

3. thirteen

    31   13

Name _____ Date _____

Counting Clouds

Write the missing numbers in each cloud.

157, _____ , 159

287, _____ , 289

349, _____ , 351

221, _____ , 223

414, _____ , 416

332, _____ , 334

399, _____ , 401

498, _____ , 500

Which dinosaur always finishes in third place?

Write the missing numbers.
Solve the riddle using your answers.

501, _____, 503	859, _____, 861
B	S
699, _____, 701	925, _____, 927
Z	D
549, _____, 551	744, _____, 746
U	O
687, _____, 689	825, _____, 827
M	N
828, _____, 830	989, _____, 991
R	A
906, _____, 908	998, _____, 1,000
T	E

Solve the Riddle! Write the letter that goes with each number.

_____ _____ _____ _____ _____ _____ -
502　829　745　826　700　999

_____ _____ _____ _____ _____ _____ _____
990　860　990　550　829　550　860

Name _____ Date _____

Which side of a house gets the most rain?

Count by 5s. Write the missing numbers.
Solve the riddle using your answers.

10, 15, 20, _____ E	45, 50, 60, _____ I
30, 35, 40, _____ N	15, 20, 25, _____ S
40, 45, 50, _____ T	25, 30, 35, _____ F
60, 65, 70, _____ R	35, 40, 45, _____ U
80, 85, 90, _____ O	85, 90, 95, _____ D
55, 60, 65, _____ H	75, 80, 85, _____ B

Solve the Riddle! Write the letter that goes with each number.

_____ _____ _____
55   70   25

_____ _____ _____ _____ _____ _____ _____
95   50   55   30   65   100   25

Skip-Counting Caterpillars

Each of these caterpillars is skip-counting by a different number. Can you figure out what each one is counting by? Fill in the numbers that they have missed.

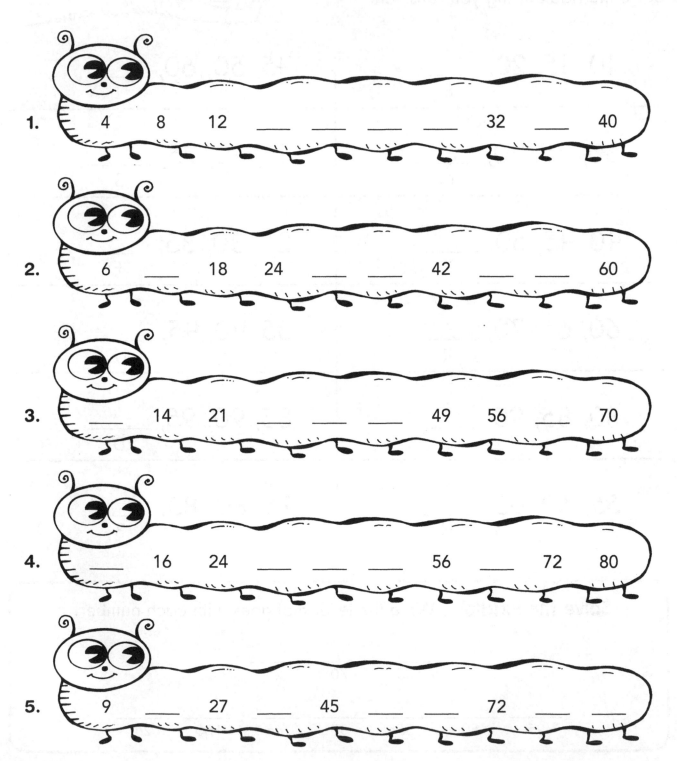

1. 4   8   12   ___   ___   ___   32   ___   40

2. 6   ___   18   24   ___   42   ___   ___   60

3. ___   14   21   ___   ___   49   56   ___   70

4. ___   16   24   ___   ___   56   ___   72   80

5. 9   ___   27   ___   45   ___   72   ___

Name _____ Date _____

What do friendly cats say to each other?

Count down by 5s. Write the missing numbers.
Solve the riddle using your answers.

20, 15, 10, ____	55, 50, 45, ____
A	V
40, 35, 30, ____	25, 20, 15, ____
Y	N
50, 45, 40, ____	35, 30, 25, ____
J	H
70, 65, 60, ____	45, 40, 35, ____
C	E
90, 85, 80, ____	100, 95, 90, ____
M	T
75, 70, 65, ____	65, 60, 55, ____
D	I

Solve the Riddle!   Write the letter that goes with each number.

____ ____ ____ ____   ____
20   5   40   30   5

____ ____ ____ ____   ____ ____ ____ .
75   50   55   30   60   5   25

Name _____

Date _____

Carrot Cruncher

Connect the dots in order.
Start at 10. Skip-count by 10.
What picture did you make?

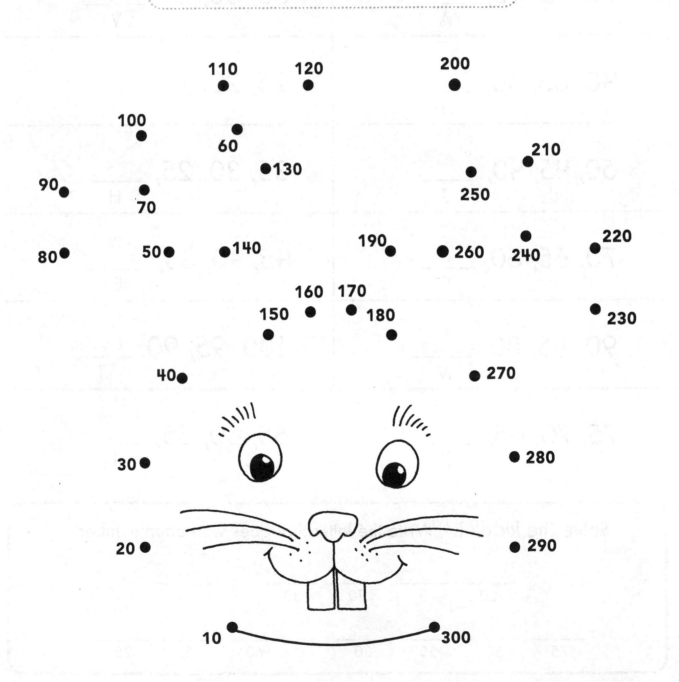

100 Math Practice Pages, Grade 2 © 2015 • Scholastic Teaching Resources

Name _____ Date _____

Odd or Even?

Circle the even numbers

Draw an X on the odd numbers.

27

46   62

93   20   81

58   34

59   15

 Quick Review _____

1. How many sets of two? _____	2. How many sets of 5? _____	3. How many sets of 3? _____
	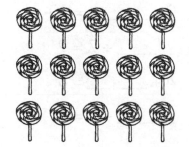	

100 Math Practice Pages, Grade 2 © 2015 • Scholastic Teaching Resources

I've Got Your Number!

Answer three problems in a row to get Tic-Tac-Math!

Fill in the missing numbers.

424 _____ 426 _____

_____ _____ 430

_____ 432 _____

On the back of this paper, draw these colors in the order listed.

- A red line first
- A yellow line last
- A blue line second
- A green line third

This is a doubles fact:

$$2 + 2 = 4$$

Write three more doubles facts.

What is:

- 10 more than 6? _____
- 10 more than 59? _____
- 10 more than 210? _____
- 10 more than 629? _____

This domino shows 9.

Make three more dominoes that show 9.

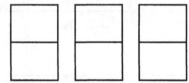

Write some odd numbers.

_____ _____ _____ _____

_____ _____ _____

Circle the largest number you wrote.

Solve.

15 – 5 = _____

14 – 4 = _____

13 – 3 = _____

12 – 2 = _____

11 – 1 = _____

Fill in the missing numbers.

2 + _____ = 10

_____ + 7 = 9

4 + _____ = 8

_____ + 2 = 7

	7	
1		3

Use these numbers to make:

- the smallest 3-digit number. _____
- the largest 3-digit number. _____

Name _____ Date _____

Fishy Fun

Find the answer to each problem.

If the number has a	Color the space
1 or 3 in the ones place	Orange
2 or 3 in the hundreds place	Yellow
1 or 2 in the thousands place	Red

Color Key

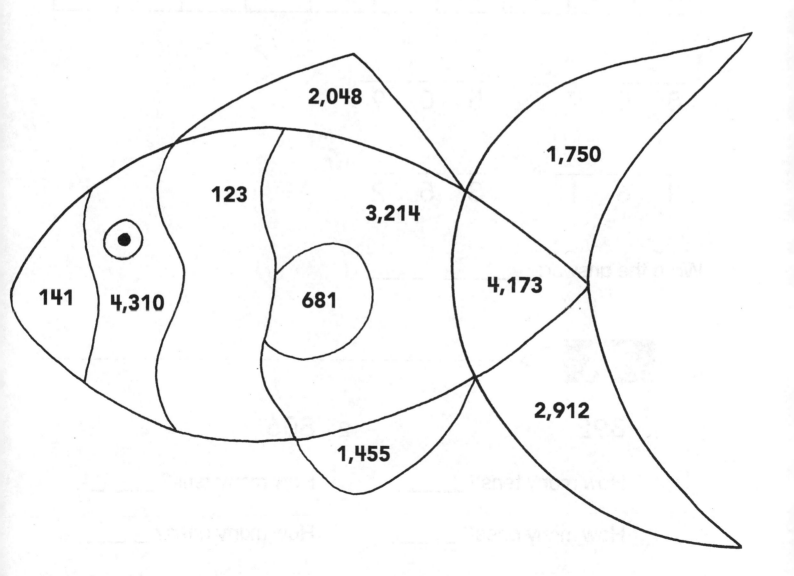

It's Your Birthday!

Decode the mystery question.

Circle each number in the tens place.

Write the letter on the line that goes with each circled number.

A	D	E	H	L	O	R	U	W	Y
1,145	93	319	84	801	52	64	720	276	1,731

8 5 7   5 0 9

___ ___ ___   ___ ___ ___ ?

4 6 1   3 5 2

Write the answer: _____

1. 392

   How many tens? _____

   How many ones? _____

2. 806

   How many tens? _____

   How many ones? _____

Name _____ Date _____

Ready, Set, Go!

Help each car get to the Finish line.
Find the answer to each problem.

If the number has a	Color the box and trace the connecting lines
4 or 7 in the tens place	Blue
1 or 5 in the hundreds place	Green
2 or 3 in the thousands place	Red

Color Key

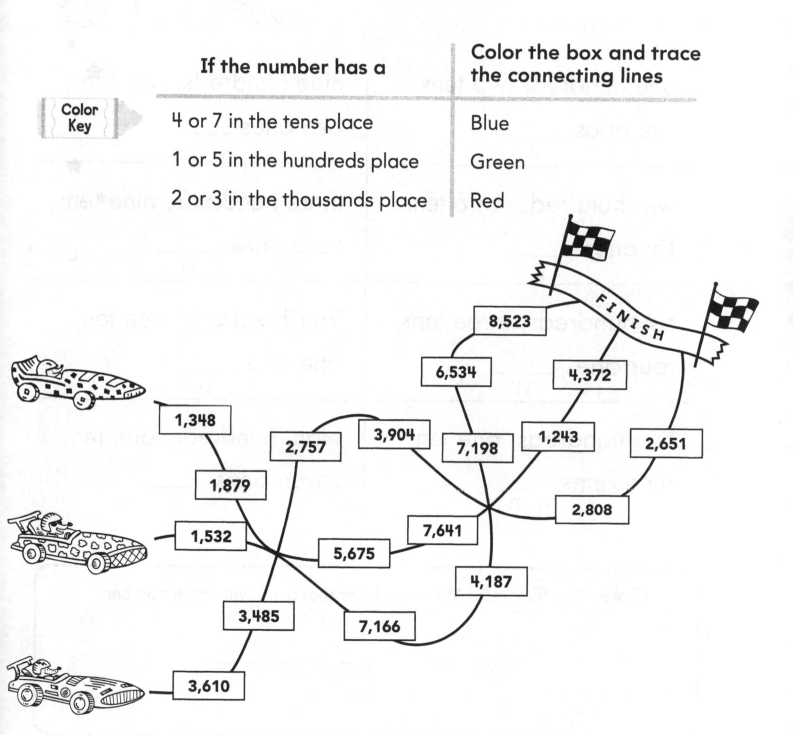

Name _____   Date _____

What runs but never walks?

Read the words and write the number.
Solve the riddle using your answers.

one hundred, two tens, five ones _____ A	nine hundreds, two tens, two ones _____ C
two hundreds, zero tens, six ones _____ E	three hundreds, nine tens, zero ones _____ N
six hundreds, three tens, four ones _____ W	four hundreds, one ten, one one _____ D
five hundreds, one ten, nine ones _____ T	eight hundreds, one ten, seven ones _____ R

Solve the Riddle! Write the letter that goes with each number.

____ ____ ____ ____ ____
634   125   519   206   817

100 Math Practice Pages, Grade 2 © 2015 • Scholastic Teaching Resources

Name _____ Date _____

Number Hunt

Greta picked a mystery number.

Use the chart and clues to find the number.

The number is:

- an odd number

- greater than 71

- less than 75

Color Greta's mystery number.

61	62	63	64	65	66	67	68	69	70
71	72	73	74	75	76	77	78	79	80
81	82	83	84	85	86	87	88	89	90

Quick Review

Compare the numbers.
Write > or < on each line.

1. 77 _____ 71   2. 62 _____ 82   3. 90 _____ 79

4. 88 _____ 89   5. 45 _____ 54   6. 31 _____ 18

100 Math Practice Pages, Grade 2 © 2015 • Scholastic Teaching Resources

Name _____ Date _____

Yum, Yum, Gum!

If the number is	Color the space
> 100 and < 250	Yellow
> 250 and < 400	Red
> 400 and < 550	Orange
> 550 and < 600	Green
> 600 and < 750	Purple

Color Key

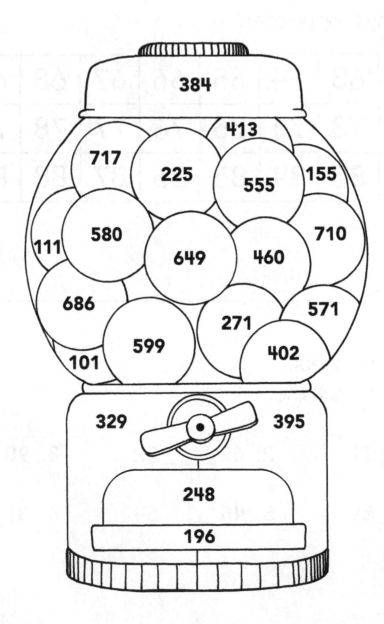

What is black and white and green?

Add.

Solve the riddle using your answers.

6 8 + 2 ___ P	9 4 + 1 ___ S	9 6 + 3 ___ B	2 4 + 7 ___ I	5 6 + 4 ___ Z	2 4 + 1 ___ U
2 3 + 4 ___ E	4 4 + 3 ___ C	5 8 + 4 ___ K	5 4 + 3 ___ T	3 1 + 6 ___ R	4 3 + 1 ___ A

Solve the Riddle! Write the letter that goes with each number.

___ ___ ___ ___ ___ ___ ___ ___
8   14   9   8   14   13   11   17

___ ___ ___ ___ ___
15   9   18   10   8

100 Math Practice Pages, Grade 2 © 2015 • Scholastic Teaching Resources

Billy's Baseball Caps

Look at the sum in the middle of each hat tree.
Then help Billy fill in the numbers on his caps.
He wants the three numbers on each side of the
tree to add up to the sum in the middle. Use only
the numbers in the key. For each tree, the numbers
on two caps have already been filled in.

Hint: A number cannot be used more than once
on each tree.

KEY		
1	2	3
4	5	6

Name _____ Date _____

A New Sport

Fill in words and numbers as directed. Then solve the problem.

A new sport has been created in the

country of _____ Land.
<small>(last name of a famous person)</small>

It is called _____ ball.
<small>(name of a body part)</small>

To play, you need a very

_____
<small>(adjective)</small>

_____. When the referee blows the whistle,
<small>(noun)</small>

you must try to _____ the _____
<small>(present-tense verb)</small>   <small>(same noun)</small>

into the goal. There are _____ goalies and
<small>(single-digit number greater than 1)</small>

_____ defensive players on a team. There are
<small>(single-digit number greater than 1)</small>

also _____ offensive players. Everyone wears
<small>(single-digit number greater than 1)</small>

_____ when they play. This is for their protection,
<small>(type of clothing, plural)</small>

of course. It is a pretty _____ game!
<small>(adjective)</small>

Solve This!

How many players are on a
team in this new sport? _____

What word has the most letters?

Add.
Solve the riddle using your answers.

15 + 10 ___ O	63 + 10 ___ M	41 + 10 ___ R	36 + 10 ___ X	64 + 10 ___ Y	51 + 10 ___ D
28 + 10 ___ F	80 + 10 ___ L	79 + 10 ___ A	58 + 10 ___ B	47 + 10 ___ N	26 + 10 ___ I

Solve the Riddle! Write the letter that goes with each number.

___ ___ ___ ___ ___ ___ ___
73   89   36   90   68   25   46

Name _____ Date _____

Super Sums

Find each sum.

1. 805 + 100 = _____

2. 697 + 100 = _____

3. 1,100 + 100 = _____

4. 1,391 + 100 = _____

5. 1,501 + 100 = _____

 **Quick Review** _____

Write the number.

1. |||| ||||
   |||| ||||
   ||||

2. |||| ||||
   |||| ||||
   |||

3. |||| ||||
   |||| ||||
   |||| ||

_____   _____   _____

Name _____   Date _____

How does a lion like his steak?

Add.
Solve the riddle using your answers.

$\begin{array}{r}5\\+\ 5\\\hline\end{array}$	$\begin{array}{r}7\\+\ 7\\\hline\end{array}$	$\begin{array}{r}10\\+\ 10\\\hline\end{array}$	$\begin{array}{r}6\\+\ 6\\\hline\end{array}$	$\begin{array}{r}13\\+\ 13\\\hline\end{array}$	$\begin{array}{r}15\\+\ 15\\\hline\end{array}$
B	E	U	N	I	L
$\begin{array}{r}19\\+\ 19\\\hline\end{array}$	$\begin{array}{r}25\\+\ 25\\\hline\end{array}$	$\begin{array}{r}21\\+\ 21\\\hline\end{array}$	$\begin{array}{r}9\\+\ 9\\\hline\end{array}$	$\begin{array}{r}12\\+\ 12\\\hline\end{array}$	$\begin{array}{r}8\\+\ 8\\\hline\end{array}$
D	O	R	F	M	A

Solve the Riddle!   Write the letter that goes with each number.

___ ___ ___ ___ ___ ___   ___ ___ ___ ___
24 14 38 26 20 24   42 50 16 42

Colorful Calico

Find the answer to each problem.

If the answer is between	Color the space
0 and 25	Black
26 and 50	Orange
51 and 75	Brown
76 and 100	Blue

Color Key

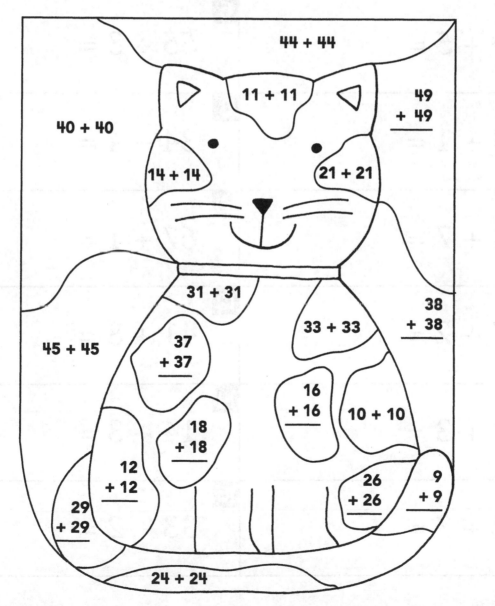

100 Math Practice Pages, Grade 2 © 2015 • Scholastic Teaching Resources

Name _____ Date _____

 # Starry Math

Add. Put a star next to all even answers.

1 30 + 2 =	**2** 23 + 6 =
3 47 + 1 =	**4** 42 + 5 =
5 50 + 5 =	**6** 55 + 3 =
7 28 + 1 =	**8** 34 + 4 =
9 61 + 7 =	**10** 67 + 1 =
11 77 + 2 =	**12** 41 + 8 =
13 54 + 3 =	**14** 14 + 3 =
15 22 + 7 =	**16** 33 + 2 =

Name _____ Date _____

What candies do scientists like best?

Add.

Solve the riddle using your answers.

42 + 7 A	33 + 5 R	10 + 9 E	12 + 4 D	25 + 2 T	14 + 0 X
46 + 1 S	24 + 2 I	32 + 3 P	41 + 1 L	21 + 8 M	36 + 1 N

Solve the Riddle! Write the letter that goes with each number.

___ ___ ___ ___ ___ ___ **-** ___ ___ ___ ___ ___
19 14 35 19 38 26   29 26 37 27 47

Name _____ Date _____

It All Adds Up!

Add. Circle the greatest sum and the least sum.

1.
```
   34
+  43
```

2.
```
   27
+  62
```

3.
```
   45
+  34
```

4.
```
   42
+  55
```

5.
```
   50
+  15
```

6.
```
   55
+  13
```

7.
```
   38
+  21
```

8.
```
   74
+  24
```

9.
```
   61
+  17
```

10.
```
   67
+  20
```

11.
```
   77
+  12
```

12.
```
   41
+  28
```

Fancy Restaurant

Fill in words and numbers as directed. Then solve the problem.

My cousin _____ won
(name of a boy)

an essay contest. The prize was dinner with

_____! They went to a fancy
(name of a famous person)

restaurant called the _____ _____ .
(adjective)   (noun)

My cousin ordered fried _____ . It only cost
(type of food)

_____ dollars. _____
(double-digit number using any combination of 1, 2, 3, or 4)   (name of the same famous person)

ordered _____ _____ . That cost
(adjective)   (type of food)

_____ dollars and came with fried
(double-digit number using any combination of 1, 2, 3, or 4)

_____ . After dinner, they went _____ .
(type of food, plural)   (verb ending in -ing)

My cousin had a really _____ time!
(adjective)

Solve This!   How much money did the
two meals cost altogether? _____

Math Around Town

All around town, people are using math.
Read each problem carefully.
Then solve.

1

Walid is making a family album. So far, he has 26 photos
of his parents. He also has 73 photos of his brothers
and sisters. How many photos are in Walid's album?

_____ photos

2

A school chorus has 25 girls and 23 boys.
How many total singers are in the chorus?

_____ girls

3

Van A has seats for 15 riders. Van B has seats for
16 riders. Van C has seats for 14 riders. How many seats
are in Vans A and C?

_____ seats

4

Lola picks 3 baskets of limes. One basket has 25 limes.
Another basket has 22 limes. The third basket has 20 limes.
How many limes has Lola picked in all?

_____ limes

To the Top

Can you add your way to the top of these towers? Add each pair of side-by-side numbers together. Write their sum in the box directly above the pair. Continue to add each pair until you reach the top of the tower.

Example:

```
            14
         8    6      ----- 8 + 6 = 14
3 + 5 = 8 ---- 3  5  1  ---- 5 + 1 = 6
```

1.
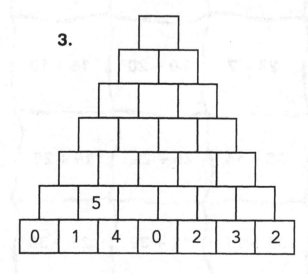

2.
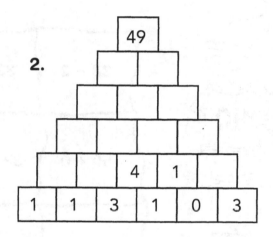

3.
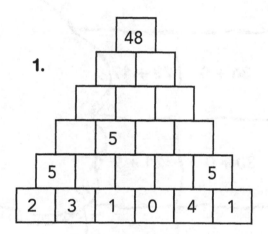

4.
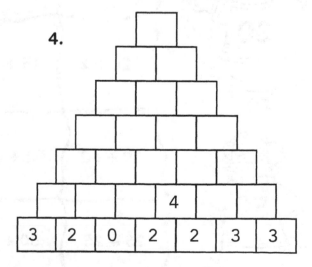

Name _____

Date _____

A Cool Swim

Help each penguin get to the iceberg.
Find the answer to each problem.

If the answer is	Color the space
30	Yellow
40	Green
50	Blue

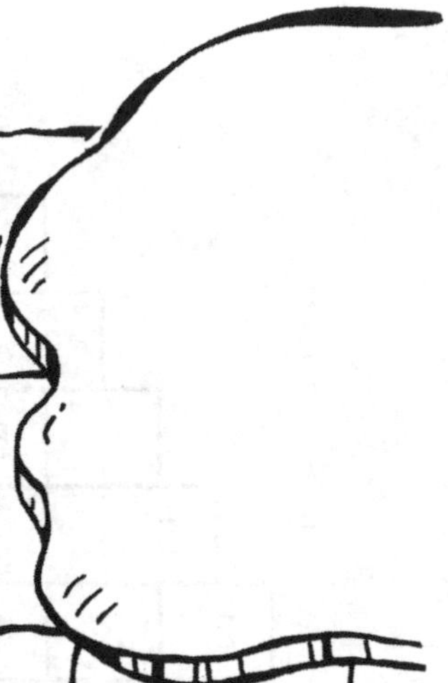

Color Key

38 + 2	33 + 7	36 + 4	23 + 17	
40 + 0	32 + 43	30 + 0	21 + 9	
52 + 0	11 + 51	22 + 8	44 + 6	22 + 28
28 + 2	15 + 15	23 + 7	30 + 20	16 + 10
10 + 60	42 + 22	35 + 16	26 + 24	14 + 29
25 + 25	50 + 0	35 + 15	11 + 39	33 + 33

40

30

50

Cheese, Please

Can you help this little mouse find its way through the maze of equations to reach the cheese? To get from the start of the maze to the end of the maze, shade in only those boxes with equations that have a sum that is even. You may move across (→), down (↓), or diagonally (↘).

ODD AND EVEN NUMBERS

* When two even numbers are added, the sum is always even.

* When an even number and an odd number are added, the sum is always odd.

* When two odd numbers are added, the sum is always even.

Start

20 + 2	9 + 10	5 + 4	18 + 3	35 + 5	4 + 9
44 + 6	22 + 15	41 + 8	62 + 8	34 + 17	28 + 2
13 + 1	43 + 3	66 + 5	33 + 1	44 + 9	52 + 6
52 + 3	38 + 6	88 + 11	12 + 4	27 + 6	21 + 9
39 + 22	17 + 7	8 + 2	10 + 53	62 + 45	55 + 11
71 + 24	55 + 34	28 + 19	82 + 17	29 + 36	99 + 1

Finish

Math Cheers

Give me
a S-U-M!

1. Add. Circle two sums that are the same.

```
   13          61          39
 + 54        + 17        + 50
```

```
   44          53          27
 + 53        + 16        + 42
```

2. Add. Regroup as needed. Circle the greatest sum.

```
   48          75          51
 + 36        + 16        + 39
```

```
   36          40          94
 + 49        + 82        + 53
```

Playful Pup

Playful Pup ripped up Davy's addition homework! To help Davy put his problems back together, find the sum for each equation. Then draw a line to the torn piece of paper that has the matching sum. Use the back of the page to show how you got your answers.

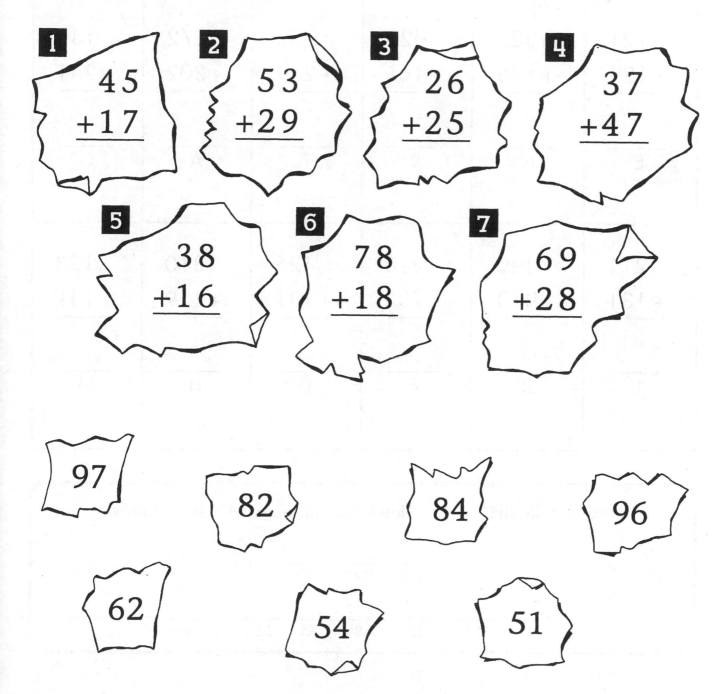

1.
$$45 + 17$$

2.
$$53 + 29$$

3.
$$26 + 25$$

4.
$$37 + 47$$

5.
$$38 + 16$$

6.
$$78 + 18$$

7.
$$69 + 28$$

97

82

84

96

62

54

51

Name _____ Date _____

What happens once in every minute, twice in every moment, but not once in a hundred years?

Add.
Solve the riddle using your answers.

121 +124 ⎯⎯ E	322 +145 ⎯⎯ N	420 +166 ⎯⎯ R	104 +264 ⎯⎯ T	272 +302 ⎯⎯ A	131 +251 ⎯⎯ O
211 +131 ⎯⎯ L	140 +413 ⎯⎯ B	210 +235 ⎯⎯ F	126 +131 ⎯⎯ D	310 +119 ⎯⎯ H	123 +141 ⎯⎯ M

Solve the Riddle! Write the letter that goes with each number.

___ ___ ___
368 429 245

___ ___ ___ ___ ___ ___ ___
342 245 368 368 245 586 264

Name _____ Date _____

Slither and Slide

Find the answer to each problem.

If the answer is between	Color the space
100 and 400	Purple
400 and 700	Blue
700 and 1,000	Green

Color Key

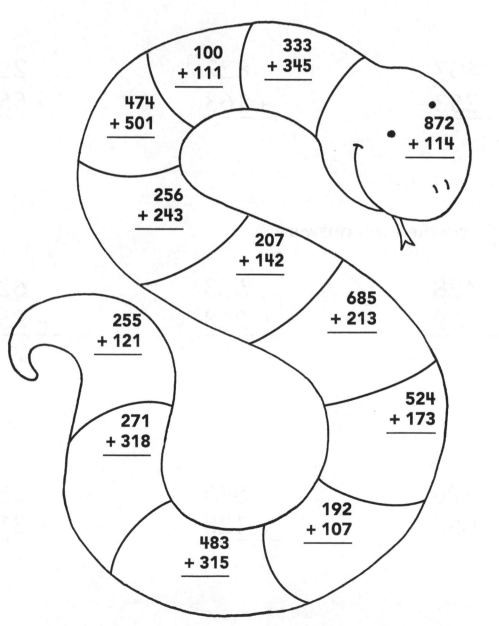

100
+ 111

333
+ 345

474
+ 501

872
+ 114

256
+ 243

207
+ 142

685
+ 213

255
+ 121

524
+ 173

271
+ 318

192
+ 107

483
+ 315

100 Math Practice Pages, Grade 2 © 2015 • Scholastic Teaching Resources

Ready, Set, Regroup!

1. Add. Circle the greatest sum and the least sum.

343	635	386
+517	+145	+504

407	827	234
+253	+163	+556

2. Add. Circle the even answers.

428	523	627
+ 359	+ 268	+ 254

308	545	369
+ 456	+ 128	+ 315

Name _____ Date _____

What is a computer's favorite snack?

Add.

Solve the riddle using your answers.

227 +285 ___ O	189 +266 ___ C	267 +346 ___ B	166 +168 ___ A	275 +245 ___ P	149 +179 ___ M
274 +129 ___ I	129 +186 ___ H	488 +139 ___ L	162 +189 ___ S	388 +149 ___ R	128 +288 ___ N

Solve the Riddle! Write the letter that goes with each number.

__ __ __ __ __ **-** __ __ __ __ __
328 403 455 537 512   455 315 403 520 351

Name _____ Date _____

Regrouping Rodeo

Add. Circle the greatest sum.

1.
$$\begin{array}{r} 165 \\ + 176 \\ \hline \end{array}$$

2.
$$\begin{array}{r} 445 \\ + 638 \\ \hline \end{array}$$

3.
$$\begin{array}{r} 501 \\ + 299 \\ \hline \end{array}$$

4.
$$\begin{array}{r} 425 \\ 239 \\ + 141 \\ \hline \end{array}$$

5.
$$\begin{array}{r} 285 \\ 312 \\ + 164 \\ \hline \end{array}$$

6.
$$\begin{array}{r} 303 \\ 181 \\ + 545 \\ \hline \end{array}$$

7.
$$\begin{array}{r} 316 \\ 481 \\ + 352 \\ \hline \end{array}$$

8.
$$\begin{array}{r} 257 \\ 193 \\ + 212 \\ \hline \end{array}$$

9.
$$\begin{array}{r} 514 \\ 368 \\ + 207 \\ \hline \end{array}$$

Name _____ Date _____

All Kinds of Math

Answer three problems in a row to get Tic-Tac-Math!

67 42 + 11 ——	208 + 802 ——	255 + 99 ——
Fill in the blank to make each equation true. $8 +$ ____ $= 15$ ____ $+ 9 = 25$ $17 + 18 =$ ____ ____ $+ 25 = 45$	**If you saw 3 birds in a tree, how many legs would there be?** _____ legs	**Read the clues to figure out the mystery number.** • 3 groups of 6 • 1 ten and 8 ones • 2 less than 20 • one dozen plus 6 The mystery number is _____.
Are the equations equal? $5 + 2 = 8 - 1$ yes no $10 - 1 = 3 + 3$ yes no $9 - 2 = 9 + 2$ yes no $10 + 1 = 3 + 7$ yes no	**One goldfish at the pet store costs 20 cents. How much do 4 goldfish cost?** _____ cents	**Sue is 5 years old. Kelsey is 3 years older than Sue.** How old is Kelsey? _____ years old How old will Kelsey be in 10 years? _____ years old

Name _____ Date _____

Clowning Around

Help each clown subtract 10 to find the missing answer.

1 82 − 10 = ◯

2 63 − 10 = ◯

3 57 − 10 = ◯

4 42 − 10 = ◯

5 78 − 10 = ◯

6 99 − 10 = ◯

Name _____ Date _____

High Flyer

Write the answer for each problem.
Connect the dots in the order of your answers.
What picture did you make?

a. $27 - 3 =$ ☐

b. $66 - 5 =$ ☐

c. $17 - 12 =$ ☐

d. $71 - 71 =$ ☐

e. $45 - 32 =$ ☐

f. $59 - 2 =$ ☐

g. $83 - 21 =$ ☐

h. $79 - 7 =$ ☐

i. $54 - 30 =$ ☐

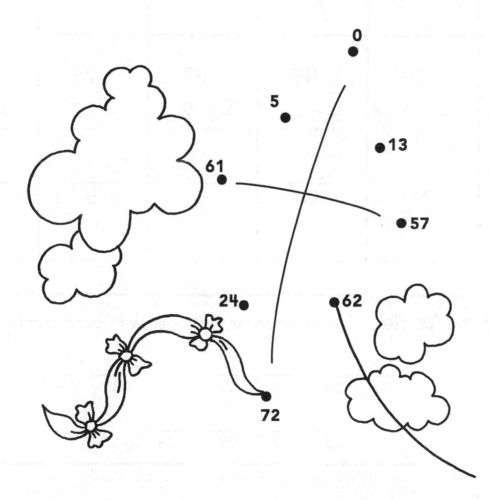

Name _____

Date _____

What kind of dog likes to do the washing?

Subtract.

Solve the riddle using your answers.

15 − 3 —— U	18 − 5 —— M	29 − 9 —— A	37 − 31 —— E	55 − 2 —— D	44 − 14 —— V
54 − 3 —— L	24 − 2 —— N	49 − 3 —— O	37 − 2 —— R	28 − 17 —— B	39 − 5 —— T

Solve the Riddle! Write the letter that goes with each number.

___ ___ ___ ___ ___ ___ ___ ___ **-**
20   51   20   12   22   53   35   46

___ ___ ___ ___
13   12   34   34

Name _____ Date _____

Robot Builders

Fill in words and numbers as directed. Then solve the problem.

The twins, _____
(first name that starts with a *J*)

and _____
(first name that starts with a *J*)

_____, decided
(last name that starts with a *J*)

to build a robot. They wanted it to be

able to _____ and
(present-tense verb)

_____.
(present-tense verb)

They thought that would be helpful around the house. They found a

_____ with _____ bolts in
(type of container)   (single-digit number greater than 4)

it. They used _____ bolts to build the robot. They
(choose a number: 2, 3, or 4)

powered the robot with _____ and gave it a test
(plural noun)

run. Their robot worked so well, they decided to name it the Amazing

_____ Robot.
(adjective)

Solve This!

How many bolts did the
twins have left after
they built the robot? _____

100 Math Practice Pages, Grade 2 © 2015 • Scholastic Teaching Resources

Subtraction Ahoy!

Read each problem
carefully. Then float on
by to solve them.

1

It's a sunny, windy day and there are 16 sailboats on the bay. If 3 boats return to shore, how many are still sailing?

2

A flock of 25 seagulls are flying overhead. If 5 seagulls land on a boat, how many are still flying?

3

It's a busy morning on the pier! There are 19 people trying to catch fish. By noon, 7 people catch fish and go home. How many people are still fishing?

4

Along the shore, 12 children are flying kites. Two children return to their family picnic for lunch. How many children are still flying kites?

100 Math Practice Pages, Grade 2 © 2015 • Scholastic Teaching Resources

Name _____ Date _____

What kind of dinosaur is always ready for bed?

Subtract.
Solve the riddle using your answers.

74	86	93	57	64	99
−51	−42	−12	−22	−22	−36
J	T	A	R	W	M

54	83	98	63	92	83
−22	−22	−14	−13	−22	−10
E	N	P	X	S	U

Solve the Riddle! Write the letter that goes with each number.

___ ___ ___ ___ ___ ___ ___ -
81 84 81 23 81 63 81

___ ___ ___ ___ ___ ___ ___ ___ ___ ___
70 81 73 35 73 70   35 32 50

Name _____

Date _____

Space Subtraction

Solve the problem in each spaceship. Then draw a line from
the spaceship to the alien with the matching answer. Color
the alien and the spaceship the same color.

1.
$$78 - 35$$

2.
$$39 - 12$$

3.
$$67 - 16$$

4.
$$54 - 42$$

5.
$$65 - 43$$

6.
$$44 - 33$$

7.
$$86 - 52$$

8.
$$97 - 24$$

73

22

51

43

11

27

12

34

Name _____ Date _____

Unusual Bowling Game

Fill in words and numbers as directed. Then solve the problem.

I've started a new type of bowling.

I use _____
(double-digit number; each digit greater than 4)

pins. I put them about _____
(number greater than 1)

feet away from me.

They have to be arranged in the shape of a perfect _____.
(type of shape)

I wear _____ on my feet and put a big
(type of shoe)

_____ on my hand. The last time I played, I rolled
(noun)

_____ times and left only _____
(number greater than 1)   (double-digit number; each digit less than 5)

pins standing. I was very _____ that day!
(adjective)

Solve This! How many pins did the bowler knock down? _____

Name _____ Date _____

Greater Than or Less Than?

Complete each subtraction problem. Then fill in the box with >, <, or = to compare the answers.

1.
$$\begin{array}{r} 61 \\ -\ 56 \\ \hline \end{array}$$ □ $$\begin{array}{r} 72 \\ -\ 29 \\ \hline \end{array}$$

2.
$$\begin{array}{r} 44 \\ -\ 27 \\ \hline \end{array}$$ □ $$\begin{array}{r} 45 \\ -\ 28 \\ \hline \end{array}$$

3.
$$\begin{array}{r} 57 \\ -\ 39 \\ \hline \end{array}$$ □ $$\begin{array}{r} 63 \\ -\ 45 \\ \hline \end{array}$$

4.
$$\begin{array}{r} 71 \\ -\ 48 \\ \hline \end{array}$$ □ $$\begin{array}{r} 98 \\ -\ 59 \\ \hline \end{array}$$

5.
$$\begin{array}{r} 83 \\ -\ 34 \\ \hline \end{array}$$ □ $$\begin{array}{r} 74 \\ -\ 26 \\ \hline \end{array}$$

6.
$$\begin{array}{r} 92 \\ -\ 78 \\ \hline \end{array}$$ □ $$\begin{array}{r} 85 \\ -\ 67 \\ \hline \end{array}$$

 100 Math Practice Pages, Grade 2 © 2015 • Scholastic Teaching Resources

Name _____ Date _____

Math-O-Matic

Each of Amanda's Math-O-Matic machines subtracts the number put into it from the number shown on the machine. To show how each machine works, fill in the number on the blank ball. Then write an equation in the boxes. The first one has been done for you.

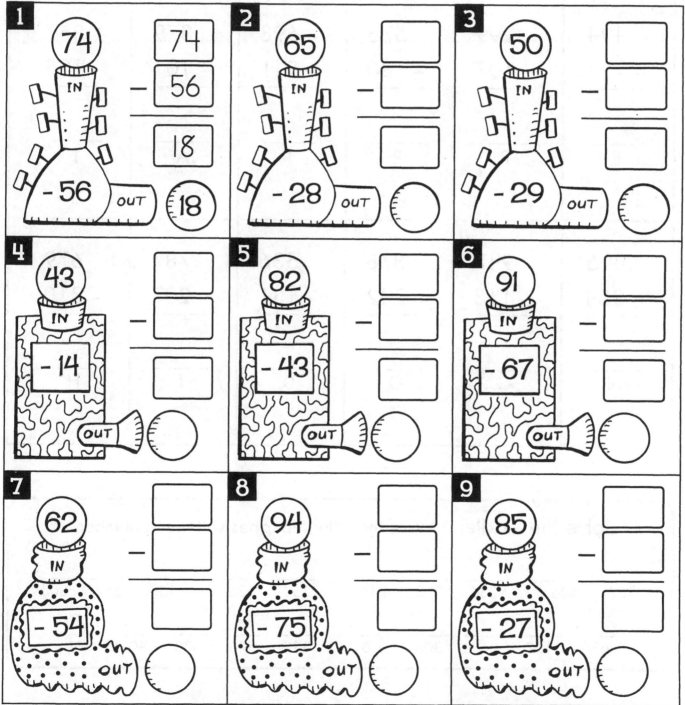

1.
74
IN
− 56   OUT   18

74
− 56
———
18

2.
65
IN
− 28   OUT

3.
50
IN
− 29   OUT

4.
43
IN
− 14   OUT

5.
82
IN
− 43   OUT

6.
91
IN
− 67   OUT

7.
62
IN
− 54   OUT

8.
94
IN
− 75   OUT

9.
85
IN
− 27   OUT

Why is this lion crossing the road?

Subtract.

Solve the riddle using your answers.

424 − 121 ___ E	299 − 107 ___ P	576 − 130 ___ R	698 − 541 ___ T	379 − 101 ___ A	867 − 125 ___ L
445 − 234 ___ N	947 − 113 ___ G	878 − 242 ___ O	536 − 131 ___ D	787 − 207 ___ I	679 − 310 ___ H

Solve the Riddle! Write the letter that goes with each number.

157 636 ___ 834 303 157 ___ 157 636 ___ 157 369 303

636 157 369 303 446 ___ 192 446 580 405 303

Name _____ Date _____

Big Bloom

Find the answer to each problem.

If the answer is between	Color the space
0 and 199	Orange
200 and 399	Yellow
400 and 599	Brown
600 and 799	Blue

Color Key

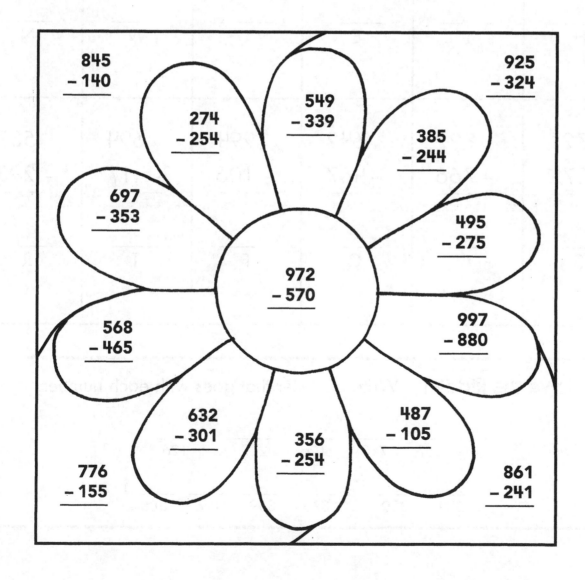

100 Math Practice Pages, Grade 2 © 2015 • Scholastic Teaching Resources

Name _____ Date _____

What did the trees say on the first day of spring?

Subtract.

Solve the riddle using your answers.

952 − 234 ─── H	721 − 346 ─── L	868 − 529 ─── E	562 − 459 ─── Y	935 − 278 ─── W	826 − 357 ─── N
721 − 279 ─── S	892 − 766 ─── A	642 − 467 ─── C	994 − 106 ─── F	694 − 417 ─── T	537 − 293 ─── R

Solve the Riddle!   Write the letter that goes with each number.

___ ___ ___ ___   ___
657 718 126 277   126

___ ___ — ___ ___ ___ ___!
244 339   375 339 126 888

Name _____ Date _____

Soaring With Subtraction

Subtract. Circle the greatest difference.

1. $\begin{array}{r} 867 \\ -597 \\ \hline \end{array}$

2. $\begin{array}{r} 648 \\ -175 \\ \hline \end{array}$

3. $\begin{array}{r} 719 \\ -365 \\ \hline \end{array}$

4. $\begin{array}{r} 936 \\ -486 \\ \hline \end{array}$

5. $\begin{array}{r} 585 \\ -294 \\ \hline \end{array}$

6. $\begin{array}{r} 404 \\ -122 \\ \hline \end{array}$

7. $\begin{array}{r} 864 \\ -317 \\ \hline \end{array}$

8. $\begin{array}{r} 672 \\ -445 \\ \hline \end{array}$

9. $\begin{array}{r} 836 \\ -408 \\ \hline \end{array}$

10. $\begin{array}{r} 761 \\ -528 \\ \hline \end{array}$

11. $\begin{array}{r} 575 \\ -239 \\ \hline \end{array}$

12. $\begin{array}{r} 823 \\ -716 \\ \hline \end{array}$

100 Math Practice Pages, Grade 2 © 2015 • Scholastic Teaching Resources

Name _____ Date _____

Which witch turns off the lights?

Subtract.
Solve the riddle using your answers.

464 − 127 ___ S	748 − 239 ___ I	418 − 196 ___ T	687 − 159 ___ C	415 − 174 ___ A	386 − 189 ___ H
539 − 396 ___ E	913 − 147 ___ K	633 − 159 ___ R	977 − 219 ___ L	831 − 189 ___ G	423 − 238 ___ W

Solve the Riddle! Write the letter that goes with each number.

___ ___ ___   ___ ___ ___ ___ ___ ___
222 197 143   758 509 642 197 222 337

___ ___ ___ ___ ___
185 509 222 528 197

Name _____ Date _____

Plus or Minus?

Should you add or subtract? You'll have to look at the sign! Solve three problems in a row to get Tic-Tac-Math!

382 + 165	583 − 287	845 + 305
63 − 18	438 − 254	91 + 59
612 − 97	299 + 93	923 − 531

The Sign Snatcher

Snarg the sign snatcher has taken away the plus and minus signs from each of these equations. Can you put the correct ones back in? Put a plus or a minus sign in each of the boxes.

· EXAMPLE ·

15 ☐ 5 ☐ 1 = 11 ➡ 15 $-$ 5 $+$ 1 = 11

1. 5 ☐ 5 ☐ 10 = 20

2. 7 ☐ 2 ☐ 10 = 19

3. 8 ☐ 3 ☐ 5 = 10

4. 16 ☐ 1 ☐ 2 = 13

5. 100 ☐ 100 ☐ 50 = 50

6. 42 ☐ 4 ☐ 2 = 48

7. 78 ☐ 2 ☐ 10 = 70

8. 15 ☐ 3 ☐ 2 = 14

Hint
Check your answers by trying the equations after you've put in the signs.

Bonus! Now try this even more challenging equation.

330 ☐ 110 ☐ 4 = 224

Name _____ Date _____

Three Little Pigs

**Fill in words and numbers as directed.
Then solve the problem.**

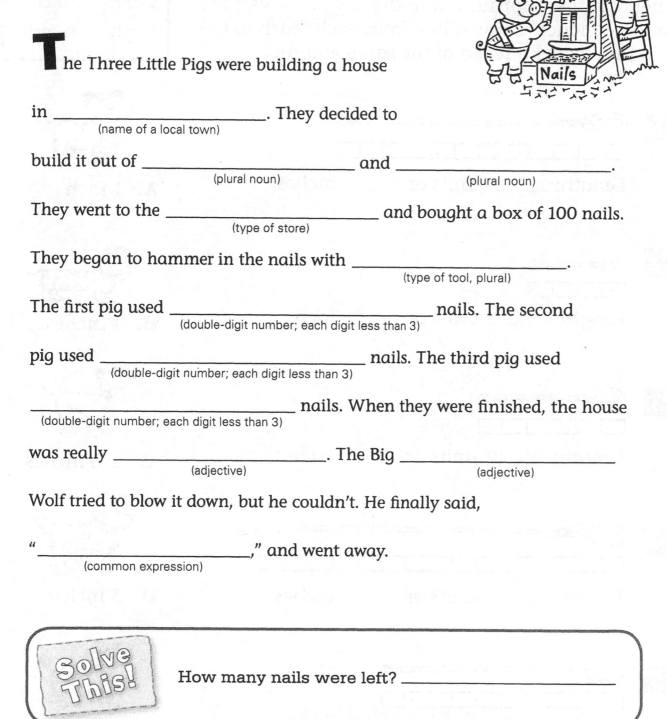

The Three Little Pigs were building a house

in _____. They decided to
(name of a local town)

build it out of _____ and _____.
(plural noun)   (plural noun)

They went to the _____ and bought a box of 100 nails.
(type of store)

They began to hammer in the nails with _____.
(type of tool, plural)

The first pig used _____ nails. The second
(double-digit number; each digit less than 3)

pig used _____ nails. The third pig used
(double-digit number; each digit less than 3)

_____ nails. When they were finished, the house
(double-digit number; each digit less than 3)

was really _____. The Big _____
(adjective)   (adjective)

Wolf tried to blow it down, but he couldn't. He finally said,

"_____," and went away.
(common expression)

Solve This!

How many nails were left? _____

100 Math Practice Pages, Grade 2 © 2015 • Scholastic Teaching Resources

Name _____ Date _____

Let's Go for a Walk!

It's time to go for a walk, but the Tiny Town dogs have mixed up their leashes. To match the dogs to their leashes, write the length of each leash in units. Then use the information in the key to convert the units to inches. Draw a line from each leash to the dog that wears a leash of the same length.

KEY
4 units = 1 inch
2 units = ½ inch

1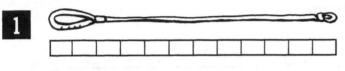

Length: _____ units or _____ inches

A. 1 inch

2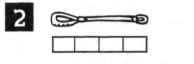

Length: _____ units or _____ inch

B. 4 inches

3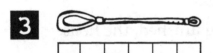

Length: _____ units or _____ inches

C. 2 ½ inches

4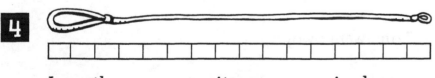

Length: _____ units or _____ inches

D. 3 inches

5

Length: _____ units or _____ inches

E. 1 ½ inches

100 Math Practice Pages, Grade 2 © 2015 • Scholastic Teaching Resources

Name _____ Date _____

Toy Math

How many inches tall is each item? Write the answer.

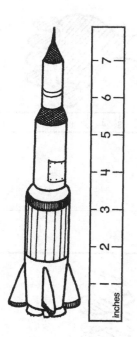

1. _____
inches tall

2. _____
inches tall

3. _____
inches tall

Quick Review

1. Circle the
   tallest one.

2. Circle the
   shortest one.

Name _____ Date _____

Animal Tracks

For each problem, write an equation on the line to show how to find the difference. Then answer the question.

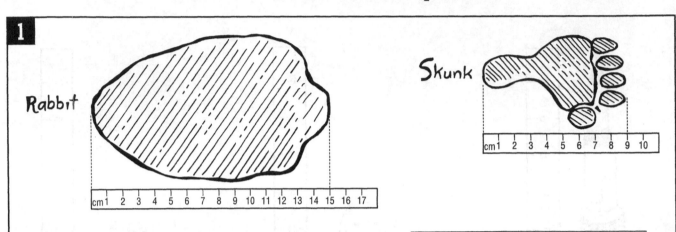

1
Rabbit
Skunk

_____

How much longer is the rabbit track? _____ cm

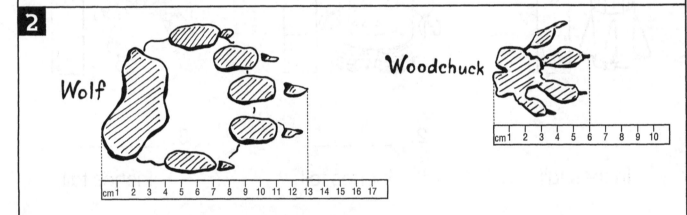

2
Wolf
Woodchuck

_____

How much longer is the wolf track? _____ cm

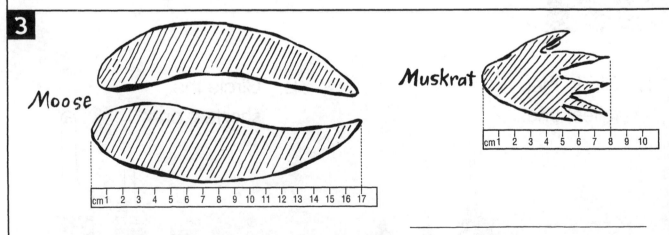

3
Moose
Muskrat

_____

How much longer is the moose track? _____ cm

Name _____ Date _____

Easy Estimations

Find each object in your classroom or home. Estimate the length of the object in inches. Then use a ruler to check your estimate. Write your answers. Compare your estimate to the actual length to see if your estimate was correct.

1

Estimate: The glue stick is about _____ inches long.

Measure: The glue stick is actually _____ inches long.

2

Estimate: The marker is about _____ inches long.

Measure: The marker is actually _____ inches long.

3

Estimate: My shoe is about _____ inches long.

Measure: My shoe is actually _____ inches long.

4

Estimate: The crayon is about _____ inches long.

Measure: The crayon is actually _____ inches long.

5

Estimate: My hand is about _____ inches long.

Measure: My hand is actually _____ inches long.

6

Estimate: The scissors are about _____ inches long.

Measure: The scissors are actually _____ inches long.

Measurement Match-Ups

Draw a line from a measurement in the left column to one in the right column that is equal in length.

1. 24 inches	**a.** 6 inches
2. 6 feet	**b.** 4 yards
3. 18 inches	**c.** 9 feet
4. 36 inches	**d.** 2 feet
5. 12 feet	**e.** 4 feet
6. 60 inches	**f.** $\frac{1}{3}$ foot
7. 4 inches	**g.** 1½ feet
8. 3 yards	**h.** 2 yards
9. 48 inches	**i.** 5 feet
10. ½ foot	**j.** 1 yard

• A Silly Riddle •

How many feet are in a yard?

Answer: That depends on how many people are standing in it.

Tiny Train Town

Use a ruler to find the measurement of each
item. Write your answers on the lines.

1

The train is __5__ inches long. The train is __1__ inch tall.

2

The tree is __1__ inch wide.

The tree is __3__ inches tall.

3

The station is __2__ inches wide.

The station is __2__ inches tall.

4

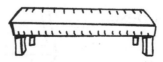

The bench is __1.5__ inches long.

The bench is __.5__ inch tall.

$\frac{1}{2}$
$\frac{1}{2}$

100 Math Practice Pages, Grade 2 © 2015 • Scholastic Teaching Resources

Name _____ Date _____

Playground Math

Solve each word problem.
Show your work in the tank.

1. Linn has a rope 9 feet long. Kenya has a rope 7 feet long. The girls lay the ropes end-to-end. What is the total length?

_____ feet

2. Casey is a good baseball player. He threw a baseball 87 feet. Fern's best throw was 15 feet shorter. How far did Fern's best throw go?

_____ feet

It Takes Time

Look at the pictures in each box.
Circle the activity that takes the most time.

1	2
3	4
5	6

Name _____   Date _____

What kind of cookie do termites like best?

Circle the time that makes the most sense.
Solve the riddle using your answers.

My alarm clock rings in the morning at 7:15 A.M. 7:15 P.M. A D	I get home from school at 3:30 A.M. 3:30 P.M. C M
I do my homework at 5:00 A.M. 5:00 P.M. H N	We eat lunch at 12:10 A.M. 12:10 P.M. B E
The sun rises at 5:45 A.M. 5:45 P.M. O R	Mom had an early meeting at 7:00 A.M. 7:00 P.M. L Y
I go to bed at 8:30 A.M. 8:30 P.M. U T	Our class meeting is at 9:10 A.M. 9:10 P.M. K I

Solve the Riddle! Write the letter that goes with each time.

___ ___ ___ ___ — ___ ___ ___
5:45 A.M. 7:15 A.M. 9:10 A.M.   3:30 P.M. 12:10 P.M. 7:15 A.M. 7:00 A.M.

Saturday Morning

This is how Tim spends Saturday mornings.

Use the table to write each time in the story. The first one has been done for you.

What I Do	Start Time
Wake up.	half past seven
Watch cartoons.	quarter to eight
Get dressed.	quarter to ten
Take piano lesson.	quarter after ten
Play with Sparky.	half past eleven

Tim wakes up at __7:30__ . He watches cartoons starting at

_____ . He gets dressed at _____ . His piano lesson starts

at _____ . After his lesson, Tim plays with his dog at _____ .

Then, Tim is ready for lunch!

 100 Math Practice Pages, Grade 2 © 2015 • Scholastic Teaching Resources

Time Match

Look at each clock or time phrase on the left.
Find the matching clock or time phrase on the right.
Then draw a line to connect the matching times.

a quarter past 2

11:45

ten o'clock

15 minutes past 6

100 Math Practice Pages, Grade 2 © 2015 • Scholastic Teaching Resources

What did the dog say
when he stubbed his paw?

Read the clocks. Write the times.
Solve the riddle using your answers.

: ___ O	: ___ F	: ___ T
: ___ S	: ___ L	: ___ E
: ___ N	: ___ W	: ___ I

Solve the Riddle!   Write the letter that goes with each time.

___ ___ **-** ___ ___ ___ **!**
5:05 10:45   10:45 5:05 10:45

Time for Work

Solve each word problem. Show your
work in the tank.

1. A baker starts
   work at 6:00 A.M.
   He ends work
   at 2:00 P.M.
   How many
   hours does the
   baker work?

   _____ hours

2. Hiram runs a
   hot dog stand.
   At 1:30, he left
   a sign. It said,
   "I'll be back in
   20 minutes."
   What time
   will Hiram
   get back?

   _____

Name _____ Date _____

Busy Day

Mark has a busy day! Use his schedule to answer the questions.

Mark's Schedule	
8:30 A.M.	Ride the bus to school
11:45 A.M.	Eat lunch
2:45 P.M.	School ends
3:00 P.M.	Go to after-school art program
4:15 P.M.	Ride the bus home
5:00 P.M.	Walk the dog
5:30 P.M.	Do homework
6:30 P.M.	Eat dinner
7:30 P.M.	Watch TV
8:00 P.M.	Take a bath
9:00 P.M.	Go to bed

1 When does Mark eat lunch? _____ : _____ _____

2 How much time passes between lunch and the end of school? _____

3 How much time does Mark spend at the after-school art program? _____

4 When does Mark go home? _____ : _____ _____

5 How long does Mark walk the dog? _____

6 When does Mark watch TV? _____ : _____ _____

7 How long does he watch TV? _____

Name _____ Date _____

It's About Time

Follow the directions to complete each problem.

1. Write each time with A.M. or P.M.

_____   _____   _____

2. Draw hands to show each time.

quarter to 3   half past 10   30 minutes after 5

Name _____ Date _____

Coin Combos

Priscilla has 10¢.

Circle the combination of coins that Priscilla has.

 Quick Review

Compare the value of the coins. Write >, <, or = on each line.

1.  _____

2. _____

3.  _____

100 Math Practice Pages, Grade 2 © 2015 • Scholastic Teaching Resources

Name _____ Date _____

What starts with *e*, ends with *e*, and has one letter in it?

Find the value of the coins.
Solve the riddle using your answers.

_____¢ L	_____¢ V
_____¢ E	_____¢ P
_____¢ O	_____¢ N

Solve the Riddle! Write the letter that goes with each value.

____ ____ ____ ____ ____ ____ ____ ____
15¢ 50¢ 35¢ 15¢ 6¢   11¢ 30¢ 15¢

100 Math Practice Pages, Grade 2 © 2015 • Scholastic Teaching Resources

Coin Pouch Pairs

Add the value of the coins in each pouch. Write your
answers on the lines. Then trace the strings that connect the
pairs of pouches, using a different color for each pair. Color
the pouch in each pair that has the higher value of coins.

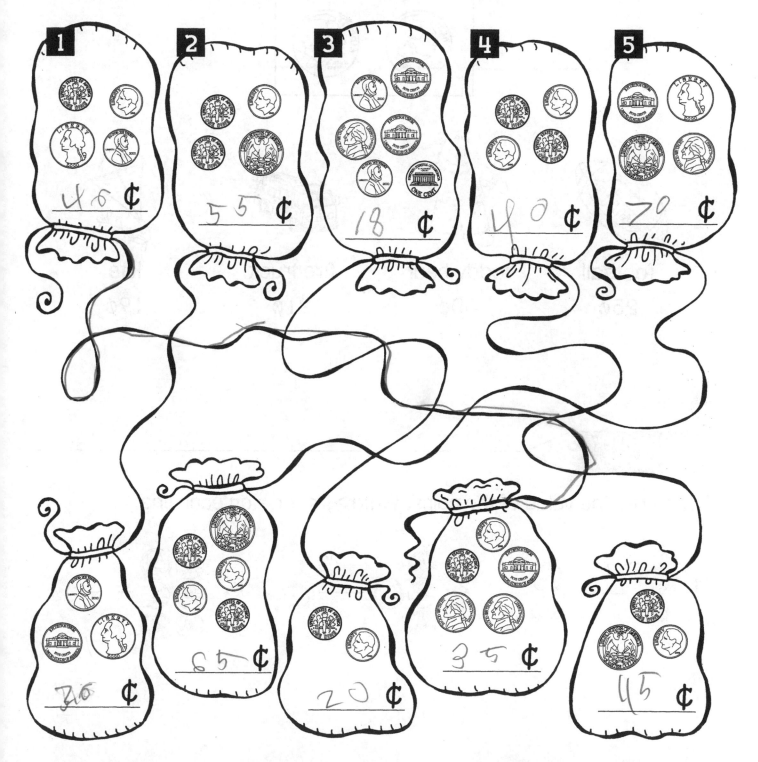

1. 40 ¢

2. 55 ¢

3. 18 ¢

4. 40 ¢

5. 70 ¢

30 ¢

65 ¢

20 ¢

35 ¢

45 ¢

Name _____ Date _____

Toy Shopping

Larry has two dimes. What can he buy with his money?

Circle the answer.

football	teddy bear	fire truck	kite
25¢	30¢	21¢	19¢

 **Quick Review**

Compare the value of the coins. Write >, <, or = on each line.

1.  7 _____

2.

3.

100 Math Practice Pages, Grade 2 © 2015 • Scholastic Teaching Resources

Name _____ Date _____

What dance do Australian animals like best?

Add the coin values.

Solve the riddle using your answers.

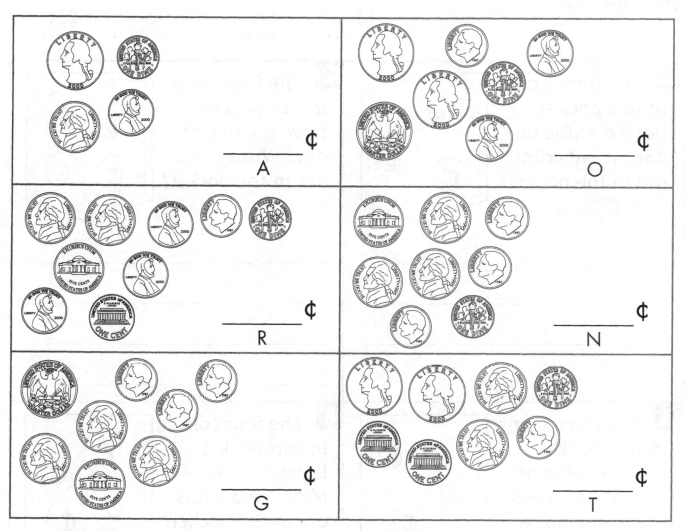

_____ ¢
A

_____ ¢
O

_____ ¢
R

_____ ¢
N

_____ ¢
G

_____ ¢
T

Solve the Riddle! Write the letter that goes with each value.

_____ _____ _____ _____ _____ — _____ _____ _____
82¢ 41¢ 60¢ 75¢ 97¢   39¢ 97¢ 97¢

100 Math Practice Pages, Grade 2 © 2015 • Scholastic Teaching Resources

Name _____ Date _____

Pocket Change

Use the information in the key to guess which coins are in each pocket. Write the coin names on the lines.

KEY

penny 1¢   nickel 5¢   dime 10¢   quarter 25¢

1 The three coins in this pocket have a value of 25¢. What coins are in the pocket?

_____
_____
_____

2 The four coins in this pocket have a value of 46¢. What coins are in the pocket?

_____
_____
_____

3 The three coins in this pocket have a value of 21¢. What coins are in the pocket?

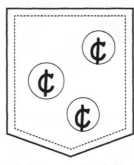

_____
_____
_____

4 The four coins in this pocket have a value of 60¢. What coins are in the pocket?

_____
_____
_____

Name _____ Date _____

Menu Math

Yummy Foods Menu

hamburger
25¢

taco
10¢

soup
15¢

pizza
20¢

salad
15¢

spaghetti
25¢

How much will each order cost? Write the answer.

1. taco and salad _____¢   3. hamburger and soup _____¢

2. two slices of pizza _____¢   4. spaghetti and salad _____¢

Quick Review

Compare the value of the coins. Write >, <, or = on each line.

1. _____   2. _____   3. _____

100 Math Practice Pages, Grade 2 © 2015 • Scholastic Teaching Resources

What's in Their Pockets?

Study the chart of coins. Then solve each word problem.

1. In one of his pockets, Jerome has 2 coins that total 30¢.

   What coins does he have? _____ and _____

2. In another pocket, he has 3 of the same kind of coin that total 15¢.

   Which coin is this? _____

3. In his jacket pocket, he has 4 coins that total 13¢.

   What coins does he have? _____ ,

   _____ , _____ , _____

4. Mandy finds 8 of the same kind of coin in one of her pockets.

   She counts $2.00! Which coin is this? _____

5. She has 4 coins that total 17¢ in her skirt pocket.

   What coins does she have? _____ ,

   _____ , _____ , _____

6. She has 3 coins that total 40¢ in her blouse pocket.

   What coins does she have? _____ , _____ ,

   _____

Name _____

Date _____

Lunchtime

Read each word problem carefully.
Then solve.

1. Dev buys a slice of pizza for $2, a salad for $2, and a drink for $5. How much money does he spend in all?

_____

2. Ruthie went to a diner for lunch. She spent $3.29 for a sandwich and $1.50 for lemonade. How much did Ruthie spend on lunch?

_____

3. Kiri bought a hamburger for $1.50, salad for $1.20, and iced tea for $1.00. How much did she spend in all?

_____

4. Eva buys a turkey wrap for $3.75. She also gets cole slaw for $1.50. She drinks water, which is free. How much does Eva spend in all?

_____

Spending Money

Read each word problem carefully.
Then solve.

1

Ruben had 13 dollars. He spent 5 dollars on a movie
ticket and 2 dollars on popcorn. How much money did
he have left?

_____ dollars

2

Jake took 5 quarters and 6 dimes to the store. He spent
85¢ on a fruit roll. He spent 50¢ on a banana. How
much money does Jake have left?

Jake has _____ left.

3

Kit has 87¢. He buys a pen for 45¢. He buys an eraser for
30¢. How much money is left?

Kit still has _____

4

Avery buys a sweater for $14. He pays with a $20 bill.
How much change does he get?

He gets _____

Where do kittens go shopping?

About how much does each item cost?
Round each price to the nearest dollar.
Circle the closest estimate.
Solve the riddle using your answers.

$1.89 each (Popcorn)		
$1.00	$2.00	$3.00
R	A	X

4:15 **$6.79 each**		
$5.00	$6.00	$7.00
L	B	O

99¢ each (flag)		
$1.00	$2.00	$3.00
N	Y	H

$4.99 each (doll)		
$4.00	$5.00	$6.00
E	G	J

$2.69 each (marbles)		
$2.00	$3.00	$4.00
K	C	Z

$8.29 (headphones)		
$7.00	$8.00	$9.00
D	I	M

$6.19 each (fire truck)		
$5.00	$6.00	$7.00
Q	L	V

$4.39 each (book)		
$4.00	$5.00	$6.00
T	S	P

Solve the Riddle!   Write the letter that goes with each value.

____ ____ ____
$8.00 $1.00 $2.00

—

____ ____ ____   ____ ____ ____ ____
$3.00 $2.00 $4.00 $2.00 $6.00 $7.00 $5.00

Name _____ Date _____

Measure for Measure

Answer three problems in a row
to get Tic-Tac-Math!

Collect some coins and put them on a table. Sort the coins according to their value.	**Write one thing that you always do in the morning.** _____ **Write one thing that you always do in the afternoon.** _____	**Which weighs less? Circle the correct answer.** crayon or shoe house or bike mouse or TV car or telephone pencil or person
What time do you: eat dinner? _____ wake up? _____ go to bed? _____ go to school? _____	**Make a chain using 5 paper clips. Look for things in the room that are about the same length as your chain.**	**If you have 7 dimes, how much money do you have?** _____ **How much is 10 cents more?** _____
Fill in the missing numbers on the clock. 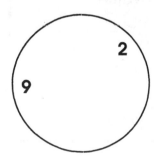	**I am thinking of a coin.** • It is silver. • It has a face on it. • It is small and thin. • It is worth ten cents. What is the name of the coin? _____	**Write the names of the months that end with -ber.** _____ _____ _____ _____

Basketball Scores

Laura plays basketball on the Red Racers team. How well did her team do? To find out, look at each scoreboard. Circle the team that won the game. On the back of the page, write a subtraction problem to show the difference in the score. Then write the correct answer on the line.

1

FINAL SCORE	
Red Racers	93
Yellow Bees	68

The game was won

by _____ points.

2

FINAL SCORE	
Silver Lightning	49
Red Racers	78

The game was won

by _____ points.

3

FINAL SCORE	
Red Racers	84
Pink Panthers	93

The game was won

by _____ points.

4

FINAL SCORE	
Blue Blizzard	106
Red Racers	114

The game was won

by _____ points.

5

FINAL SCORE	
Red Racers	85
Orange Zippers	111

The game was won

by _____ points.

6

FINAL SCORE	
Green Dragons	117
Red Racers	123

The game was won

by _____ points.

Name _____ Date _____

Take Away

Use the picture graph to answer questions about Lee's fish.

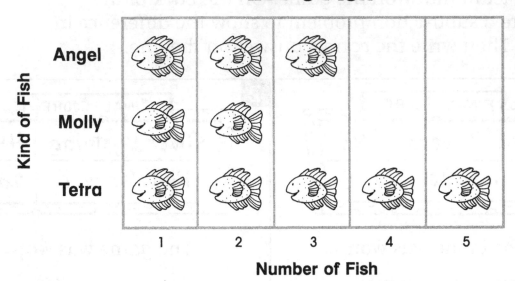

1. How many different kinds of fish does Lee have? _____

2. Lee has _____ angel fish.

3. Lee has 2 _____ fish.

4. Lee has _____ more tetra fish than angel fish.

 Quick Review

Write the number.

1. ||||| ||||| |||| 2. ||||| ||||| 3. ||||| ||||| |||||
                                                                        ||||| ||||| ||

_____   _____   _____

Name _____ Date _____

Book Math

Use the graph about favorite types of books to answer the questions.

Favorite Types of Books

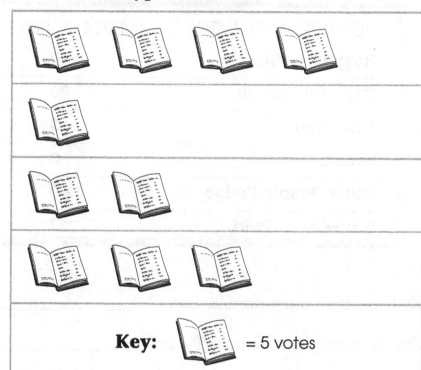

Mystery

Science Fiction

Historical Fiction

Nonfiction

Key: = 5 votes

1. What is the value of one  ? _____

2. How many people like nonfiction best? _____

3. How many people like historical fiction best? _____

4. How many people like science fiction best? _____

5. Which was the most popular type of book? _____

6. How many people picked this type of book? _____

Name _____ Date _____

Who Wants Chocolate?

Super Scoops wants to know how popular each of its ice cream flavors is. Can you help them figure it out? Here is what they sold one day:

ICE CREAM FLAVOR	NUMBER OF PINTS SOLD
Raspberry Ripple	10
Caramel Crunch	20
Mint Chip	10
Vanilla	8
Nutty Double Fudge	40
Strawberry Swirl	12

1. What was their most popular flavor? _____

2. What was their least popular flavor? _____

3. How many pints of Caramel Crunch did they sell? _____

4. What two flavors sold the same number of pints?

_____ and _____

5. How many pints of Raspberry Ripple and Strawberry Swirl did they

sell in total? _____

6. How many more pints of Strawberry Swirl than Mint Chip did

they sell? _____

7. How many pints in all did they sell? _____

8. What flavor would you buy? _____

Name _____ Date _____

Sleepy Bar Graph

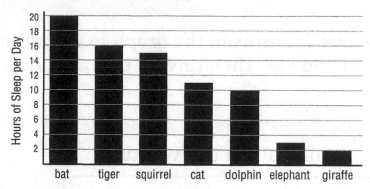

Use this bar graph to answer three problems in a row and get Tic-Tac-Math!

What does this graph show? _____ _____ _____	**Which animal sleeps the most number of hours a day?** _____ How many hours? _____	**How many hours does a squirrel sleep in a day?** _____
Which sleeps more, a tiger or a squirrel? _____	**How many more hours does a bat sleep than a cat?** _____	**Which animal sleeps the least number of hours a day?** _____ **How many hours?** _____
How many animals sleep more than 10 hours a day? _____	**Which animal sleeps only 3 hours a day?** _____	**How many hours do you sleep in a day?** _____ Add a bar on the graph showing how many hours. Label the bar with your name.

Name _____ Date _____

In the Woods

Draw check marks in the graph to show the number of each animal you see. Then answer the questions.

Animals in the Woods

Butterfly	
Crow	
Rabbit	
Squirrel	

Key: ✔ = 1 animal

1. How many animals in all? _____

2. How many animals with wings? _____

3. How many more crows than squirrels? _____

4. How many fewer rabbits than butterflies? _____

5. Which animal do you see the most? _____

Wonderful Weather

Ask ten classmates which weather they like best.

Color a box for each answer.

10				
9				
8				
7				
6				
5				
4				
3				
2				
1				
	☀ sunny	🌬 windy	🌧 rainy	❄ snowy

1. Which kind of weather do most classmates like? Circle the answer.

2. Which kind of weather do the fewest classmates like? Circle the answer.

 **Quick Review** _____

Look at the cows. Answer the questions.

How many of each?

eyes _____   legs _____

noses _____   ears _____

tails _____

   100 Math Practice Pages, Grade 2 © 2015 • Scholastic Teaching Resources

Name _____ Date _____

Math Travels

How did the students in Mr. Hay's class get to school today?

- Six took the bus.

- Five walked.

- Three rode bikes.

- Four came in cars.

First graph the data. Then answer the questions below.

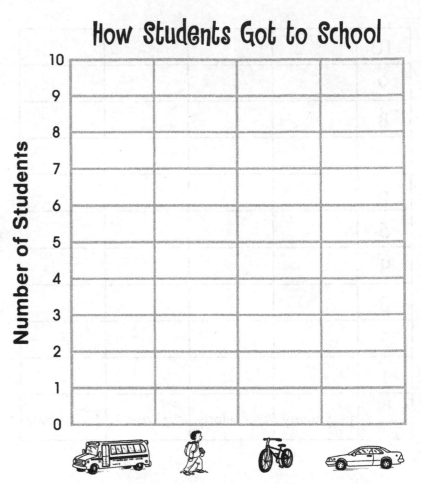

How Students Got to School

Number of Students

Way of Getting to School

1. How many students got to school today? _____

2. How many more walked than came in cars? _____

3. Which way did the most students get to school? _____

4. How many students walked or rode a bike? _____

Name _____ Date _____

Terrific Trees

Second graders helped plant trees at their school. The table shows what they planted.

Tree	Number Planted
Aspen	8
Empress	12
Poplar	10
Willow	14

Make a pictograph of the data. Write a title. Finish the key. Let △ stand for 2 trees.

_____

Key: △ = _____

Write a question about the data in the graph.

_____

_____

Name _____ Date _____

Shape Hunt

Read the clues to discover which shape belongs to each person.

Write each person's name under the correct shape.

 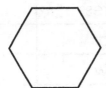

_____   _____   _____   _____   _____

●   Barb's shape has six sides.

●   Fred's shape does not have corners.

●   Deb's shape has five corners.

●   Steve's shape has more than six corners.

Which shape belongs to Chad? _____

 Quick Review

1. Color the shape with the most sides.

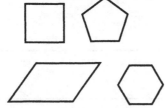

2. Color the smallest shape.

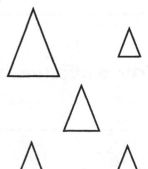

 100 Math Practice Pages, Grade 2 © 2015 • Scholastic Teaching Resources

Name _____ Date _____

Scrambled Shapes

Unscramble the shape words. Use the word bank to check your spelling.

1. bceu _____

2. enoc _____

3. quarse _____

4. crilec _____

5. ogentnap _____

6. vola _____

7. preesh _____

8. langerit _____

9. noxhage _____

10. grancleet _____

11. rudeliartqal _____

12. gontoca _____

WORD BANK

circle
cone
cube
hexagon
octagon
oval
pentagon
quadrilateral
rectangle
sphere
square
triangle

Name _____ Date _____

Creative Shapes

Draw a picture of something that has each shape.

circle	square
triangle	rectangle

1. Color the oval.   2. Color the star.   3. Color the heart.

Mystery Shapes

Follow the directions to complete each problem. Show your work in the tank.

1. Draw a big square in the tank. Draw a circle *inside* the square. Draw a triangle *inside* the circle.

   How many straight lines did you draw?

   _____

2. I am a solid shape. I have 6 square faces. Draw me in the tank.

   What shape am I?

   _____

Name _____   Date _____

Pizza Party

Divide the pizza in half.

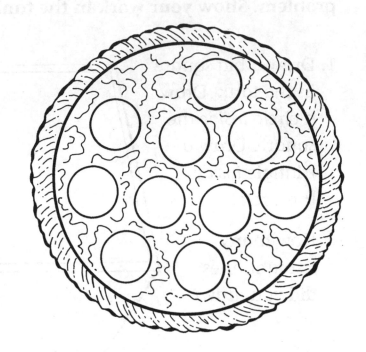

1. How many lines did you use?

   _____

2. How many slices of pizza
   did you make?

   _____

3. What fraction is each slice
   of the pizza?

   _____

4. How many friends can you
   share the pizza with?

   _____

 Quick Review _____

What fraction is the shaded area? Circle the answer.

1.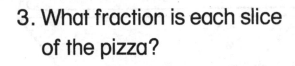

   $\frac{1}{2}$ $\frac{1}{3}$ $\frac{1}{4}$

2.

   $\frac{1}{2}$ $\frac{3}{4}$ $\frac{2}{3}$

3.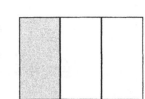

   $\frac{1}{3}$ $\frac{1}{2}$ $\frac{2}{3}$

100 Math Practice Pages, Grade 2 © 2015 • Scholastic Teaching Resources

Name _____   Date _____

Shape Show

What do the shapes show? Follow the directions below.
- Color *halves* red.
- Color *thirds* yellow.
- Color *fourths* blue.

1

2

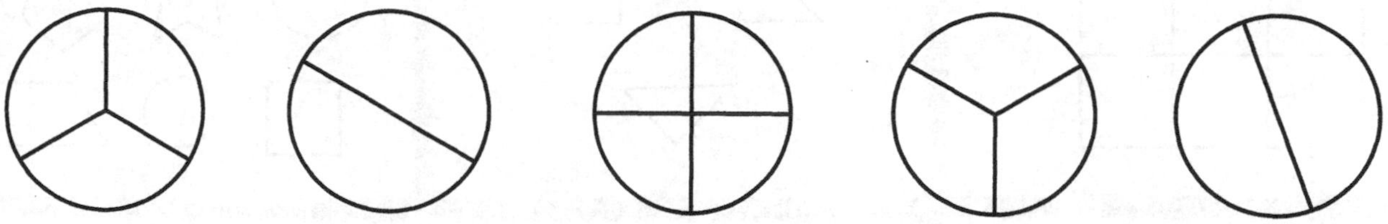

3

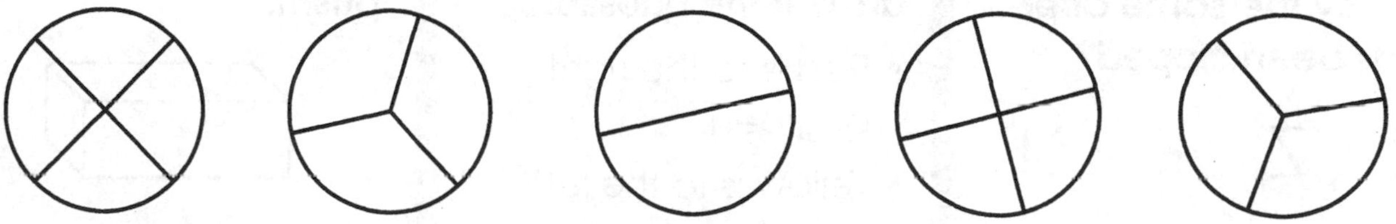

4

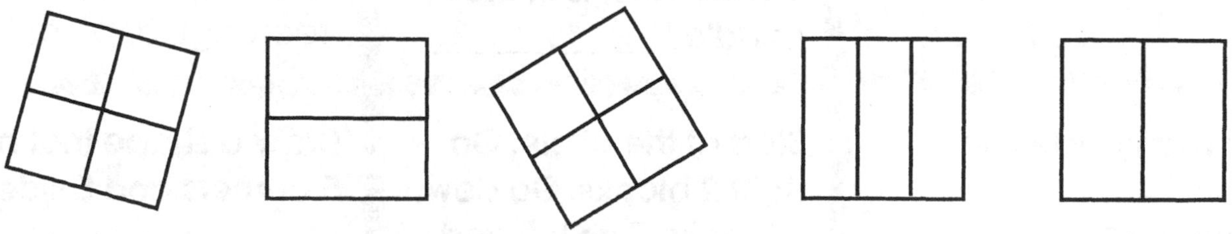

5

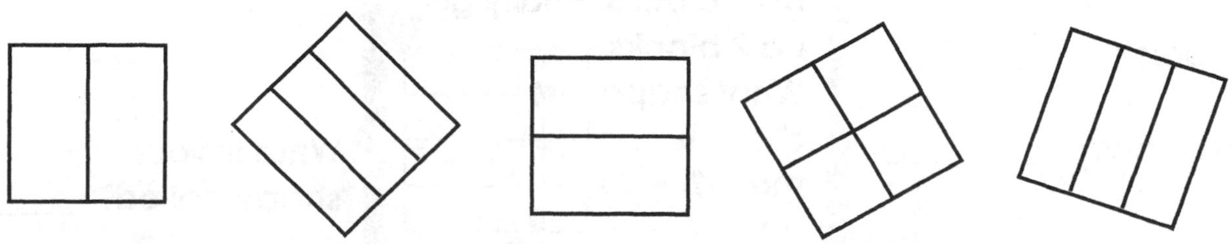

100 Math Practice Pages, Grade 2 © 2015 • Scholastic Teaching Resources

Name _____ Date _____

Not Just Shapes!

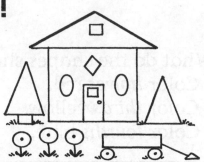

Answer three problems in a row
to get Tic-Tac-Math!

How many squares are in this drawing?

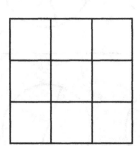

Circle the flip of this shape:

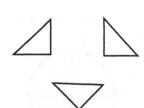

Color the shapes that are not quadrilaterals.

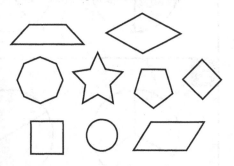

Which letter looks exactly the same after it has been flipped?

M Z F N

Read the clues. Then answer the question.

- Red is to the right of green.
- Yellow is to the left of green.

Which color is in the middle? _____

This is a rectangular prism:

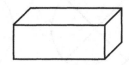

Find five things that are shaped like a rectangular prism.

How many sides on:

4 triangles? _____

3 squares? _____

2 hexagons? _____

Start at the circle. Go right 2 blocks. Go down 2 blocks. Turn left and go 2 blocks. Finally go up 2 blocks. What shape did you make?

Draw a shape that has 5 corners and 5 sides.

What is your shape called? _____

Practice Page 1:

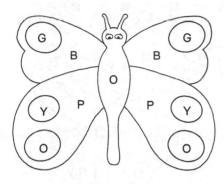

Practice Page 2:
Students should circle the 12th, 34th, 55th, and 98th bones.
Quick Review
1. 87 2. 42 3. 13

Practice Page 3:
(From left to right) 158, 288, 350, 222, 415, 333, 400, 499

Practice Page 4:
bronze-asaurus
B-502, Z-700, U-550, M-688, R-829, T-907, S-860, D-926, O-745, N-826, A-990, E-999

Practice Page 5:
the outside
E-25, N-45, T-55, R-75, O-95, H-70, I-65, S-30, F-40, U-50, D-100, B-90

Practice Page 6:
1. 16, 20, 24, 28, 36
2. 12, 30, 36, 48, 54
3. 7, 28, 35, 42, 63
4. 8, 32, 40, 48, 64
5. 18, 36, 54, 63, 81, 90

Practice Page 7:
Have a mice day.
A-5, Y-25, J-35, C-55, M-75, D-60, V-40, N-10, H-20, E-30, T-85, I-50

Practice Page 8:

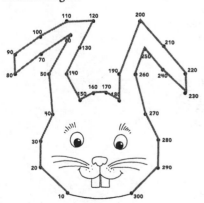

Practice Page 9:
Students should circle 20, 34, 46, 58, and 62. Students should draw an X on 15, 27, 59, 81, and 93.
Quick Review
1. 4
2. 3
3. 4

Practice Page 10:

425 427 428 429 431 433	Activity: R, B, G, Y	Answers will vary.
16 69 220 639	6, 3; 4, 5; 3, 6	Answers will vary.
10 10 10 10 10	8 2 4 5	137 731

Practice Page 11:

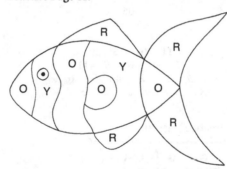

Practice Page 12:
H O W O L D A R E Y O U?
Students should write their age on the line.
Quick Review
1. 9, 2
2. 0, 6

Practice Page 13:
• Students should use blue to color the boxes with the following numbers, then use the same color to trace the line that connects these boxes:
1,348; 1,879; 5,675; 7,641; 1,243; 4,372
• Students should use green to color the boxes with the following numbers, then use the same color to trace the line that connects all of these boxes:
1,532; 7,166; 4,187; 7,198; 6,534; 8,523
• Students should use red to color the boxes with the following numbers, then use the same color to trace the line that connects all of these boxes:
3,610; 3,485; 2,757; 3,904; 2,808; 2,651

Practice Page 14:
water
A-125, E-206, W-634, T-519, C-922, N-390, D-411, R-817

Practice Page 15:
Students should color 73.
Quick Review
1. >   4. <
2. <   5. <
3. >   6. >

Practice Page 16:

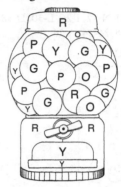

Practice Page 17:
a seasick zebra
P-16, S-14, B-18, I-13, Z-15, U-7, E-9, C-11, K-17, T-12, R-10, A-8

Practice Page 18:

Practice Page 19:
Answers will vary. Check students' work.

Practice Page 20:
mailbox
O-25, M-73, R-51, X-46, Y-74, D-61, F-38, L-90, A-89, B-68, N-57, I-36

Practice Page 21:
1. 905
2. 797
3. 1,200
4. 1,491
5. 1,601
Quick Review
1. 25
2. 23
3. 27

Practice Page 22:
medium roar
B-10, E-14, U-20, N-12, I-26, L-30, D-38, O-50, R-42, F-18, M-24, A-16

Practice Page 23:

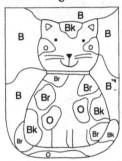

Practice Page 24:
1. 32*
2. 29
3. 48*
4. 47
5. 55
6. 58*
7. 29
8. 38*
9. 68*
10. 68*
11. 79
12. 49
13. 57
14. 17
15. 29
16. 35

Practice Page 25:
experi-mints
A-49, R-38, E-19, D-16, T-27, X-14, S-47, I-26, P-35, L-42, M-29, N-37

Practice Page 26:
1. 77
2. 89
3. 79
4. (97)
5. 65
6. 68
7. (59)
8. 98
9. 78
10. 87
11. 89
12. 69

Practice Page 27:
Answers will vary. Check students' work.

Practice Page 28:
1. 99 2. 48 3. 29 4. 67

Practice Page 29:
1.
```
            48
         24   24
      14   10   14
    9    5    5    9
  5    4    1    4    5
2    3    1    0    4    1
```
2.
```
            49
         27   22
      14   13    9
    6    8    5    4
  2    4    4    1    3
1    1    3    1    0    3
```
3.
```
             116
          58   58
       30   28   30
    15   15   13   17
  6    9    6    7   10
1    5    4    2    5    5
0    1    4    0    2    3    2
```
4.
```
             106
          46   60
       21   25   35
    11   10   15   20
  7    4    6    9   11
5    2    2    4    5    6
3    2    0    2    2    3    3
```

Practice Page 30:

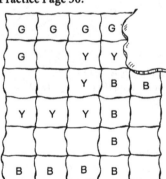

Practice Page 31:

20 + 2	9 + 10	5 + 4	18 + 3	35 + 5	4 + 9
44 + 6	22 + 15	41 + 8	62 + 8	34 + 17	28 + 2
13 + 1	43 + 3	66 + 5	33 + 1	44 + 9	52 + 6
52 + 3	38 + 6	88 + 11	12 + 4	27 + 6	21 + 9
39 + 22	17 + 7	8 + 2	10 + 53	62 + 45	55 + 11
71 + 24	55 + 34	28 + 19	82 + 17	29 + 36	99 + 1

Practice Page 32:
1. 67, 78, 89, 97, (69), (69)
2. 84, 91, 90, 85, 122, (147)

Practice Page 33:

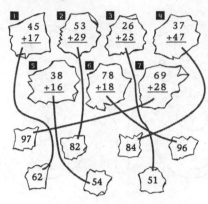

Practice Page 34:
the letter m
E-245, N-467, R-586, T-368, A-574, O-382, L-342, B-553, F-445, D-257, H-429, M-264

Practice Page 35:

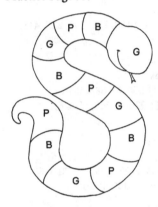

Practice Page 36:
1. (From left to right) 860, 780, 890, (660), (990), 790
2. (From left to right) 787, 791, 881, (764), 673, (684)

Practice Page 37:
micro-chips
O-512, C-455, B-613, A-334, P-520, M-328, I-403, H-315, L-627, S-351, R-537, N-416

Practice Page 38:
1. 341
2. 1,083
3. 800
4. 805
5. 761
6. 1,029
7. (1,149)
8. 662
9. 1,089

Practice Page 39:

120	1,010	354
7 16 35 20	6 legs	18
yes no no no	80 cents	8 18

Practice Page 40:
1. 72
2. 53
3. 47
4. 32
5. 68
6. 89

Practice Page 41:
a. 24
b. 61
c. 5
d. 0
e. 13
f. 57
g. 62
h. 72
i. 24

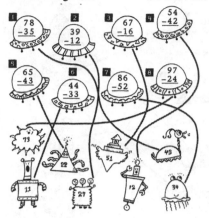

Practice Page 42:
a laundro-mutt
U-12, M-13, A-20, E-6, D-53, V-30, L-51,
N-22, O-46, R-35, B-11, T-34

Practice Page 43:
Answers will vary. Check students' work.

Practice Page 44:
1. 13
2. 20
3. 12
4. 10

Practice Page 45:
a pajama-saurus Rex
J-23, T-44, A-81, R-35, W-42, M-63, E-32,
N-61, P-84, X-50, S-70, U-73

Practice Page 46:

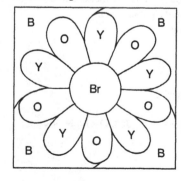

Practice Page 47:
Answers will vary. Check students' work.

Practice Page 48:
1. 5 < 43
2. 17 = 17
3. 18 = 18
4. 23 < 39
5. 49 > 48
6. 14 < 18

Practice Page 49:

1. 74 − 56 =18	2. 65 − 28 37	3. 50 − 29 21
4. 43 − 14 29	5. 82 − 43 39	6. 91 − 67 24
7. 62 − 54 8	8. 94 − 75 19	9. 85 − 27 58

Practice Page 50:
to get to the other pride
E-303, P-192, R-446, T-157, A-278, L-742,
N-211, G-834, O-636, D-405, I-580, H-369

Practice Page 51:

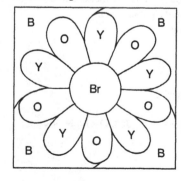

Practice Page 52:
What a re-leaf!
H-718, L-375, E-339, Y-103, W-657, N-469,
S-442, A-126, C-175, F-888, T-277, R-244

Practice Page 53:
1. 270
2. 473
3. 354
4. 450
5. 291
6. 282
7. 547
8. 227
9. 428
10. 233
11. 336
12. 107

Practice Page 54:
the lights witch
S-337, I-509, T-222, C-528, A-241, H-197,
E-143, K-766, R-474, L-758, G-642, W-185

Practice Page 55:

547	296	1,150
45	184	150
515	392	392

Practice Page 56:
1. 5 + 5 + 10 = 20
2. 7 + 2 + 10 = 19
3. 8 − 3 + 5 = 10
4. 16 − 1 − 2 = 13
5. 100 − 100 + 50 = 50
6. 42 + 4 + 2 = 48
7. 78 + 2 − 10 = 70
8. 15 − 3 + 2 = 14
BONUS—330 − 110 + 4 = 224

Practice Page 57:
Answers will vary. Check students' work.

Practice Page 58:
1. 12 units; 3 inches; Students should draw a
   line from the leash to dog D.
2. 4 units; 1 inch; Students should draw a line
   from the leash to dog A.
3. 6 units; 1 ½ inches; Students should draw a
   line from the leash to dog E.
4. 16 units; 4 inches; Students should draw a
   line from the leash to dog B.
5. 10 units; 2 ½ inches; Students should draw
   a line from the leash to dog C.

Practice Page 59:
1. 8
2. 4
3. 3
Quick Review
1. Students should circle the mop on the left.
2. Students should circle the paintbrush on the left.

Practice Page 60:
1. 15 cm – 9 cm = 6 cm; 6 cm
2. 13 cm – 6 cm = 7 cm; 7 cm
3. 17 cm – 8 cm = 9 cm; 9 cm

Practice Page 61:
Answers will vary.

Practice Page 62:
1. d
2. h
3. g
4. j
5. b
6. i
7. f
8. c
9. e
10. a

Practice Page 63:
1. 5 inches long; 1 inch tall
2. 1 inch wide; 3 inches tall
3. 2 inches wide; 2 inches tall
4. 1 ½ inches long; ½ inch tall

Practice Page 64:
1. 16 feet
2. 72 feet

Practice Page 65:
Students should circle the following:
1. child walking the dog
2. child making cookies
3. child reading a book
4. children play a game
5. child raking leaves
6. child at the movies

Practice Page 66:
oak-meal
A-7:15 A.M., M-3:30 P.M., N-5:00 P.M., E-12:10 P.M., O-5:45 A.M., L-7:00 A.M., T-8:30 P.M., K-9:10 A.M.

Practice Page 67:
7:45, 9:45, 10:15, 11:30

Practice Page 68:

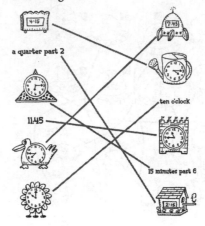

Practice Page 69:
ow-wow!
O-5:05, F-7:10, T-11:35, S-2:25, L-6:55, E-8:05, N-6:15, W-10:45, I-4:25

Practice Page 70:
1. 8 hours
2. 1:50

Practice Page 71:
1. 11:45 A.M.
2. 3 hours
3. 1 hour 15 minutes
4. 4:15 P.M.
5. 30 minutes
6. 7:30 P.M.
7. 30 minutes

Practice Page 72:
1. 2:30 A.M., 7:45 A.M., 1:15 P.M.
2. Check students' clock faces.

Practice Page 73:
Students should circle the nickel and 5 pennies (lower right corner).
Quick Review
1. <
2. >
3. >

Practice Page 74:
envelope
L-6¢, V-35¢, E-15¢, P-30¢, O-11¢, N-50¢

Practice Page 75:
1. Top pouch: 46¢; Bottom pouch; 35¢; Students should color the top pouch.
2. Top pouch: 55¢; Bottom pouch; 31¢; Students should color the top pouch.
3. Top pouch: 18¢; Bottom pouch; 20¢; Students should color the bottom pouch.
4. Top pouch: 40¢; Bottom pouch; 45¢; Students should color the bottom pouch.
5. Top pouch: 60¢; Bottom pouch; 65¢; Students should color the bottom pouch.

Practice Page 76:
Students should circle the kite.
Quick Review
1. >
2. <
3. =

Practice Page 77:
tango-roo
A-41¢, O-97¢, R-39¢, N-60¢, G-75¢, T-82¢

Practice Page 78:
1. dime, dime, nickel
2. quarter, dime, dime, penny
3. dime, dime, penny
4. quarter, quarter, nickel, nickel

Practice Page 79:
1. 25¢
2. 40¢
3. 40¢
4. 40¢
Quick Review
1. =
2. <
3. <

Practice Page 80:
1. a quarter and a nickel
2. a nickel
3. a dime, a penny, a penny, a penny
4. a quarter
5. a dime, a nickel, a penny, a penny
6. a quarter, a dime, a nickel

Practice Page 81:
1. $9
2. $4.79
3. $3.70
4. $5.25

Practice Page 82:
1. 6
2. 50¢
3. 12¢
4. $6

Practice Page 83:
in a cat-alog
A-$2.00, O-$7.00, N-$1.00, G-$5.00, C-$3.00, I-$8.00, L-$6.00, T-$4.00

Practice Page 84:

Activity	Answers will vary.	crayon bike mouse telephone pencil
Answers will vary.	Activity	70¢ 80¢
(clock showing 12:30)	dime	September, October, November, December

Practice Page 85:
1. Students should circle Red Racers; 25

$$\begin{array}{r} 93 \\ -\ 68 \\ \hline 25 \end{array}$$

2. Students should circle Red Racers; 29

$$\begin{array}{r} 78 \\ -\ 49 \\ \hline 29 \end{array}$$

3. Students should circle Pink Panthers; 9

$$\begin{array}{r} 93 \\ -\ 84 \\ \hline 9 \end{array}$$

4. Students should circle Red Racers; 8

$$\begin{array}{r} 114 \\ -\ 106 \\ \hline 8 \end{array}$$

5. Students should circle Orange Zippers; 26

$$\begin{array}{r} 111 \\ -\ 85 \\ \hline 26 \end{array}$$

6. Students should circle Red Racers; 6

$$\begin{array}{r} 123 \\ -\ 117 \\ \hline 6 \end{array}$$

Practice Page 86:
1. 3 2. 3 3. molly 4. 2
Quick Review
1. 14
2. 10
3. 27

Practice Page 87:
1. 5
2. 15
3. 10
4. 5
5. mystery
6. 20

Practice Page 88:
1. nutty double fudge
2. vanilla
3. 20 pints
4. raspberry ripple and mint chip
5. 22 pints
6. 2 pints
7. 100 pints
8. Answers will vary.

Practice Page 89:

How many hours different animals sleep in a day	bat 20 hours	15 hours
tiger	9 more hours	giraffe 2 hours
4 animals	elephant	Answers will vary.

Practice Page 90:

Butterfly	✔ ✔ ✔
Crow	✔ ✔ ✔ ✔ ✔
Rabbit	✔ ✔ ✔
Squirrel	✔ ✔

Key: ✔ = 1 animal

1. 14
2. 9
3. 3
4. 1
5. crow

Practice Page 91:
Students should color a box that corresponds to each classmate's response.
1–2. Students should use the information on their graph to answer each question.
Quick Review
4 eyes
8 legs
2 noses
4 ears
2 tails

Practice Page 92:

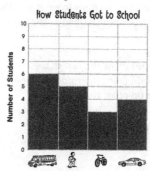

1. 18
2. 1
3. bus
4. 8

Practice Page 93:

Different Trees at School	
Aspen	△ △ △ △
Empress	△ △ △ △ △ △
Poplar	△ △ △ △ △
Willow	△ △ △ △ △ △

Key: △ = 2 trees

Title will vary.
Questions will vary.

Practice Page 94:
pentagon: Deb
hexagon: Barb
triangle: Chad
star: Steve
circle: Fred
Chad has the triangle.
Quick Review
1. Students should color the hexagon.
2. Students should color the triangle at the top right.

Practice Page 95:
1. cube
2. cone
3. square
4. circle
5. pentagon
6. oval
7. sphere
8. triangle
9. hexagon
10. rectangle
11. quadrilateral
12. octagon

Practice Page 96:
Students should draw an item in each box that corresponds to the shape named at the top of the box.
Quick Review
1. Students should color the last shape.
2. Students should color the middle shape.
3. Students should color the first shape.

Practice Page 97:
1. 7; check students' drawings.
2. cube

Practice Page 98:
1. one
2. two
3. ½
4. one
Quick Review
1. Students should circle ¼.
2. Students should circle ¾.
3. Students should circle ⅓.

Practice Page 99:
Check students' coloring.

Practice Page 100:

14 squares	△	Activity
M	green	Activity
12 12 12	square	pentagon

CPSIA information can be obtained
at www.ICGtesting.com
Printed in the USA
LVHW062130190320
650652LV00009B/146

Top Secret

Secret Service

Mark Beyer

HIGH
interest
books

Children's Press®
A Division of Scholastic Inc.
New York / Toronto / London / Auckland / Sydney
Mexico City / New Delhi / Hong Kong
Danbury, Connecticut

Michelle Innes

Photo Credits: Cover © Annie Griffiths Belt/Corbis; pp. 5, 21, 30–31
© AFP/Corbis; pp. 7, 11, 14, 28, 35 © AP/Wide World Photos;
p. 13 © R. Egan/Salt Lake Tribune/Corbis Sygma; pp. 15, 40
© Kennerly David Hume/Corbis Sygma; pp. 17, 22 © Photodisc;
p. 27 © Matthew Mendelsohn/Corbis; p. 38 © Reuters NewMedia Inc./Corbis

Library of Congress Cataloging-in-Publication Data

Beyer, Mark (Mark T.)
    The Secret Service / Mark Beyer.
    p. cm. — (Top secret)
    Summary: Describes the history, training, duties, and role of the United
States Secret Service.
    Includes bibliographical references and index.
    ISBN 0-516-24313-6 (lib. bdg.) — ISBN 0-516-24376-4 (pbk.)
    1. United States. Secret Service—Juvenile literature. 2. Secret
service—United States—Juvenile literature. [1. United States. Secret
Service. 2. Secret service. 3. Occupations.] I. Title. II. Top secret
(New York, N.Y.)

HV8144.S43 B49 2003
363.28'3'0973—dc21

                                                        2002007284